GROWING UP BLACK
was originally published by
William Morrow & Company, Inc.

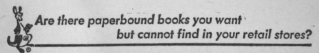

Adler, Bill comp.

GROWING UP

BLACK

EDITED BY JAY DAVID

PUBLISHED BY POCKET BOOKS NEW YORK

GROWING UP BLACK

William Morrow edition published September, 1968

A *Pocket Book* edition
1st printing.........August, 1969

Standard Book Number: 671-77093-4.
Library of Congress Catalog Card Number; 68-26436.
Copyright, ©, 1968, by William Morrow & Company, Inc.
All rights reserved. This *Pocket Book* edition is
published by arrangement with William Morrow & Company, Inc.
Printed in the U.S.A.

Acknowledgments

Grateful acknowledgment is made to:

The Viking Press, Inc., for permission to reprint material from *A Man Called White*, by Walter White. Copyright 1948 by Walter White.

David McKay Company, Inc., for permission to reprint material from *The Long Shadow of Little Rock*, by Daisy Bates. Copyright, ©, 1962, by Daisy Bates.

Hill and Wang, Inc., for permission to reprint material from *The Seeking*, by Will Thomas. Copyright 1953 by Will Thomas.

Sheed & Ward Inc., for permission to reprint material from *Dark Symphony*, by Elizabeth Laura Adams. Copyright 1942 by Sheed & Ward Inc.

Alderman Library, University of Virginia, for permission to reprint material from *Memoirs of a Monticello Slave: The Life of Isaac Jefferson*. (Original manuscript in The Tracy W. McGregor Library, University of Virginia.)

Doubleday & Company, Inc., for permission to reprint material from *His Eye Is on the Sparrow*, by Ethel Waters and Charles Samuels. Copyright 1950, 1951 by Ethel Waters and Charles Samuels.

Harper & Row, Publishers, for permission to reprint material from *A Choice of Weapons*, by Gordon Parks. Copyright, ©, 1965, 1966, by Gordon Parks.

Coward-McCann, Inc., for permission to reprint material from *Go Up for Glory*, by Bill Russell and Bill McSweeny. Copyright, ©, 1966, by William Felton Russell and William Francis McSweeny.

Grove Press, Inc., for permission to reprint material from *The Autobiography of Malcolm X*. Copyright, ©, 1964, by Alex Haley and Malcolm X. Copyright, ©, 1965, by Alex Haley and Betty Shabazz.

The Macmillan Company for permission to reprint material
  from *Manchild in the Promised Land,* by Claude Brown.
  Copyright, ©, 1965, by Claude Brown.

Harper & Row, Publishers, for permission to reprint material
  from *No Day of Triumph,* by J. Saunders Redding. Copyright 1942 by J. Saunders Redding.

Harper & Row, Publishers, for permission to reprint material
  from *Black Boy,* by Richard Wright. Copyright 1937,
  1942, 1944, 1945, by Richard Wright.

E. P. Dutton & Co., Inc., for permission to reprint material from
  the book, *Nigger: An Autobiography,* by Dick Gregory
  with Robert Lipsyte. Copyright, ©, 1964, by Dick
  Gregory Enterprises, Inc.

Harper & Row, Publishers, for permission to quote from *On
  These I Stand,* by Countee Cullen. Copyright 1925 by
  Harper & Brothers; renewed 1953 by Ida M. Cullen. (As
  quoted in *Dark Symphony,* by Elizabeth Laura Adams.)

I would like to express my sincere thanks
to my fine staff—
David Curtis, Managing Editor,
Elaine Crane, Catherine Johnston
and Janice Van Raay.

Contents

Introduction

THIS is a book about children. It is not a book written by children because the incidents were not recorded until years after they occurred. Rather, this is a book written by adults who, at some time in life, looked back to their childhood and wrote down what they remembered. What gives this anthology particular significance is the fact that the narrators are Negro adults recalling a Negro childhood.

Growing Up Black takes the reader into this dark world; it intends to offer a glimpse of what it is like to be a Negro child in America. "The child is father of the man," Wordsworth wrote; if we wish to understand behavior and attitudes of Negro adults, we should pay close attention to the formative years of childhood. In the nineteen autobiographical selections in this collection, American Negroes tell what it was and is like to grow up—as a slave in the Deep South of the early nineteenth century, as a destitute sharecropper's son in the post-Civil War period, or as a fatherless child in the brutal Northern ghettos of the mid-twentieth century. The excerpts in this collection contain a variety of experience and a great range of thought and feeling, from the tragic to the comic. But never far from the surface of any piece—if beneath the surface at all—is that single strand of community that unites the experience of all American Negroes everywhere: the bond of the oppressed.

In the words of the authors represented here are found not only nineteen moving and personal narratives, but also a history in brief of the Negro people in America. We see the slave society as it existed early in the nineteenth century, with all its cruelty, misery, and degradation. We follow the joyously liberated slaves into the Reconstruction, where their dreams of freedom and equality for a time offset the disappointing reality of their poverty. And we are there with them as they move into the twentieth century, leaving hope behind them and becoming fully aware of the desperateness of their plight. Many of the trends that modern sociologists have rendered into lifeless statistics are illuminated in all their human drama through the immediacy of the autobiographers' art. We see the sharp contrast of the mainly rural nineteenth century with the almost exclusively urban twentieth, with the consequent increased squalor, disease, and deprivation. We can also trace the gradual crumbling of the family unit, and especially the virtual disappearance of the father as the head of the family, along with the concomitant breakdown of respect for authority. And, perhaps most importantly, we can see the dawning of the Negroes' awareness of themselves as a people and as individuals, with the inevitable anger and frustration resulting from the sharpening of that perception.

Every reader will, no doubt, recognize some of the authors as prominent men and women in one field of endeavor or another. It should be understood that these selections were chosen not with the intent of recording the most extraordinary life stories, but rather with the hope of providing an index of the most common forms of Negro experience. That many of the authors later went on to achieve eminence is thus irrelevant to the stories of their childhood. In other words, it is the men and women, not their childhoods, that are remarkable.

The difficulty in dealing with relations between the races is that we tend to identify individuals with their races and thereby to avoid dealing with them as distinct human beings. It is my hope that white readers of *Growing Up Black* will suspend, if only temporarily, this tendency, and bridge the gap between themselves and the authors of the selections. Having done so, and having hopefully thus gained some insight into what being an American Negro is like, they may come to have a truer, more humane understanding of the problems at hand.

JAY DAVID
New York City

I

GROWING UP
BLACK

PROBABLY the single most important event in the life of any Negro child is his recognition of his own coloredness, with all the implications of that fact. The realization can come as mild awareness that is taken in stride, or it can come as a rude shock that results in a trauma; but whatever the circumstances, a new understanding of the self influences the child's every thought and emotion from that day forth. Truly, he sees the world through different eyes, from a different perspective, with somewhat less of the innocence of his earlier years. The selections that follow will give some idea of how a Negro child reacts to this moment of truth.

1

FROM

A Man Called White

by Walter White

(1893–1955)

Born a few years before the turn of the twentieth century, Walter White grew up in Atlanta, Georgia. His skin, like that of his parents, was so light that he could easily have passed for white. He never attempted to do so, even after the violent and bloody rioting in Atlanta in the fall of 1906 demonstrated what he had to look forward to as a Negro.

A college-educated journalist and civil rights leader, White spent most of his life trying to destroy racial prejudice.

THERE were nine light-skinned Negroes in my family: mother, father, five sisters, an older brother, George, and myself. The house in which I discovered what it meant to be a Negro was located on Houston Street, three blocks from the Candler Building, Atlanta's first skyscraper, which bore the name of the ex-drug clerk who had become a millionaire from the sale of Coca-Cola. Below us lived none but Negroes; toward town all but a very few were white. Ours was an eight-room, two-story frame

house which stood out in its surroundings not because of
its opulence but by contrast with the drabness and un-
paintedness of the other dwellings in a deteriorating
neighborhood.

Only Father kept his house painted, the picket fence
repaired, the board fence separating our place from those
on either side white-washed, the grass neatly trimmed,
and flower beds abloom. Mother's passion for neatness
was even more pronounced and it seemed to me that I
was always the victim of her determination to see no
single blade of grass longer than the others or any one
of the pickets in the front fence less shiny with paint than
its mates. This spic-and-spanness became increasingly
apparent as the rest of the neighborhood became more
down-at-heel, and resulted, as we were to learn, in sullen
envy among some of our white neighbors. It was the
violent expression of that resentment against a Negro
family neater than themselves which set the pattern of
our lives.

On a day in September 1906, when I was thirteen, we
were taught that there is no isolation from life. The un-
seasonably oppressive heat of an Indian summer day
hung like a steaming blanket over Atlanta. My sisters
and I had casually commented upon the unusual quiet-
ness. It seemed to stay Mother's volubility and reduced
Father, who was more taciturn, to monosyllables. But, as
I remember it, no other sense of impending trouble im-
pinged upon our consciousness.

I had read the inflammatory headlines in the *Atlanta
News* and the more restrained ones in the *Atlanta Constitution* which reported alleged rapes and other crimes
committed by Negroes. But these were so standard and
familiar that they made—as I look back on it now—little
impression. The stories were more frequent, however,
and consisted of eight-column streamers instead of the
usual two- or four-column ones.

Father was a mail collector. His tour of duty was from three to eleven P.M. He made his rounds in a little cart into which one climbed from a step in the rear. I used to drive the cart for him from two until seven, leaving him at the point nearest our home on Houston Street, to return home either for study or sleep. That day Father decided that I should not go with him. I appealed to Mother, who thought it might be all right, provided Father sent me home before dark because, she said, "I don't think they would dare start anything before nightfall." Father told me as we made the rounds that ominous rumors of a race riot that night were sweeping the town. . . .

During the afternoon preceding the riot little bands of sullen evil-looking men talked excitedly on street corners all over downtown Atlanta. Around seven o'clock my father and I were driving toward a mail box at the corner of Peachtree and Houston Streets when there came from near-by Pryor Street a roar the like of which I had never heard before, but which sent a sensation of mingled fear and excitement coursing through my body. I asked permission of Father to go and see what the trouble was. He bluntly ordered me to stay in the cart. A little later we drove down Atlanta's main business thoroughfare, Peachtree Street. Again we heard the terrifying cries, this time near at hand and coming toward us. We saw a lame Negro bootblack from Herndon's barber shop pathetically trying to outrun a mob of whites. Less than a hundred yards from us the chase ended. We saw clubs and fists descending to the accompaniment of savage shouting and cursing. Suddenly a voice cried, "There goes another nigger!" Its work done, the mob went after new prey. The body with the withered foot lay dead in a pool of blood on the street.

Father's apprehension and mine steadily increased during the evening, although the fact that our skins were white kept us from attack. Another circumstance favored us—the mob had not yet grown violent enough to attack United States government property. But I could see Father's relief when he punched the time clock at eleven P.M. and got into the cart to go home. He wanted to go the back way down Forsyth Street, but I begged him, in my childish excitement and ignorance, to drive down Marietta to Five Points, the heart of Atlanta's business district, where the crowds were densest and the yells loudest. No sooner had we turned into Marietta Street, however, than we saw careening toward us an undertaker's barouche. Crouched in the rear of the vehicle were three Negroes clinging to the sides of the carriage as it lunged and swerved. On the driver's seat crouched a white man, the reins held taut in his left hand. A huge whip was gripped in his right. Alternately he lashed the horses and, without looking backward, swung the whip in savage swoops in the faces of members of the mob as they lunged at the carriage determined to seize the three Negroes.

There was no time for us to get out of its path, so sudden and swift was the appearance of the vehicle. The hub cap of the right rear wheel of the barouche hit the right side of our much lighter wagon. Father and I instinctively threw our weight and kept the cart from turning completely over. Our mare was a Texas mustang which, frightened by the sudden blow, lunged in the air as Father clung to the reins. Good fortune was with us. The cart settled back on its four wheels as Father said in a voice which brooked no dissent, "We are going home the back way and not down Marietta."

But again on Pryor Street we heard the cry of the mob. Close to us and in our direction ran a stout and elderly woman who cooked at a downtown white hotel. Fifty yards behind, a mob which filled the street from curb to curb was closing in. Father handed the reins to me and, though he was of slight stature, reached down and lifted the woman into the cart. I did not need to be told to lash the mare to the fastest speed she could muster.

The church bells tolled the next morning for Sunday service. But no one in Atlanta believed for a moment that the hatred and lust for blood had been appeased. Like skulls on a cannibal's hut the hats and caps of victims of the mob the night before had been hung on the iron hooks of telegraph poles. None could tell whether each hat represented a dead Negro. But we knew that some of those who had worn hats would never again wear any.

Later in the afternoon friends of my father's came to warn of more trouble that night. They told us that plans had been perfected for a mob to form on Peachtree Street just after nightfall to march down Houston Street to what the white people called "Darktown," three blocks or so below our house, to "clean out the niggers." There had never been a firearm in our house before that day. Father was reluctant even in those circumstances to violate the law, but he at last gave in at Mother's insistence.

We turned out the lights, as did all our neighbors. No one removed his clothes or thought of sleep. Apprehension was tangible. We could almost touch its cold and clammy surface. Toward midnight the unnatural quiet was broken by a roar that grew steadily in volume. Even today I grow tense in remembering it.

Father told Mother to take my sisters, the youngest of them only six, to the rear of the house, which offered more protection from stones and bullets. My brother George was away, so Father and I, the only males in the house, took our places at the front windows. The windows opened on a porch along the front side of the house, which in turn gave onto a narrow lawn that sloped down to the street and a picket fence. There was a crash as Negroes smashed the street lamp at the corner of Houston and Piedmont Avenue down the street. In a very few minutes the vanguard of the mob, some of them bearing torches, appeared. A voice which we recognized as that of the son of the grocer with whom we had traded for many years yelled, "That's where that nigger mail carrier lives! Let's burn it down! It's too nice for a nigger to live in!" In the eerie light Father turned his drawn face toward me. In a voice as quiet as though he were asking me to pass him the sugar at the breakfast table, he said, "Son, don't shoot until the first man puts his foot on the lawn and then—don't you miss!"

In the flickering light the mob swayed, paused, and began to flow toward us. In that instant there opened within me a great awareness; I knew then who I was. I was a Negro, a human being with an invisible pigmentation which marked me a person to be hunted, hanged, abused, discriminated against, kept in poverty and ignorance, in order that those whose skin was white would have readily at hand a proof of their superiority, a proof patent and inclusive, accessible to the moron and the idiot as well as to the wise man and the genius. No matter how low a white man fell, he could always hold fast to the smug conviction that he was superior to two-thirds of the world's population, for those two-thirds were not white.

It made no difference how intelligent or talented my millions of brothers and I were, or how virtuously we lived. A curse like that of Judas was upon us, a mark of degradation fashioned with heavenly authority. There were white men who said Negroes had no souls, and who proved it by the Bible. Some of these now were approaching us, intent upon burning our house.

Theirs was a world of contrasts in values: superior and inferior, profit and loss, cooperative and noncooperative, civilized and aboriginal, white and black. If you were on the wrong end of the comparison, if you were inferior, if you were noncooperative, if you were aboriginal, if you were black, then you were marked for excision, expulsion, or extinction. I was a Negro; I was therefore that part of history which opposed the good, the just, and the enlightened. I was a Persian, falling before the hordes of Alexander. I was a Carthaginian, extinguished by the Legions of Rome. I was a Frenchman at Waterloo, an Anglo-Saxon at Hastings, a Confederate at Vicksburg. I was defeated, wherever and whenever there was a defeat.

Yet as a boy there in the darkness amid the tightening fright, I knew the inexplicable thing—that my skin was as white as the skin of those who were coming at me.

The mob moved toward the lawn. I tried to aim my gun, wondering what it would feel like to kill a man. Suddenly there was a volley of shots. The mob hesitated, stopped. Some friends of my father's had barricaded themselves in a two-story brick building just below our house. It was they who had fired. Some of the mobsmen, still bloodthirsty, shouted, "Let's go get the nigger." Others, afraid now for their safety, held back. Our friends, noting the hesitation, fired another volley. The mob broke and retreated up Houston Street.

In the quiet that followed I put my gun aside and tried to relax. But a tension different from anything I had ever known possessed me. I was gripped by the knowledge of my identity, and in the depths of my soul I was vaguely aware that I was glad of it. I was sick with loathing for the hatred which had flared before me that night and come so close to making me a killer; but I was glad I was not one of those who hated; I was glad I was not one of those made sick and murderous by pride. I was glad I was not one of those whose story is in the history of the world, a record of bloodshed, rapine, and pillage. I was glad my mind and spirit were part of the races that had not fully awakened, and who therefore still had before them the opportunity to write a record of virtue as a memorandum to Armageddon.

It was all just a feeling then, inarticulate and melancholy, yet reassuring in the way that death and sleep are reassuring, and I have clung to it now for nearly half a century.

2

FROM

The Long Shadow of Little Rock

by Daisy Bates

(1919?–   )

"If Jesus is like the white people, I don't want any part of him!" cries young Daisy Gatson in the following selection. In the context of the highly religious Negro community in southern Arkansas, and coming from a child, this is a shocking declaration, indeed. But it gives evidence to the depth of the bitterness and disillusionment a Negro child can reach when confronted with reality. With a child's simplicity but a quite adult steadfastness, she launches her drive to gain revenge for her mother's murder. The story of her gradual destruction of the guilty "Drunken Pig" is so passionately elemental and somehow distinctively Southern that it seems to belong in the pages of a William Faulkner novel.

Daisy Lee Gatson was told by her stepfather when she was a child to "hate discrimination that eats away at the soul of every black man and woman. Hate the insults and then try to do something about it or your hate won't spell a thing." Daisy followed his advice and as Mrs. L. C. Bates, Arkansas State President of the NAACP, was large-

ly responsible for the successful integration of Little Rock High School in 1957.

I WAS born Daisy Lee Gatson in the little sawmill town of Huttig, in southern Arkansas. The owners of the mill ruled the town. Huttig might have been called a sawmill plantation for everyone worked for the mill, lived in houses owned by the mill, and traded at the general store run by the mill.

The hard, red clay streets of the town were mostly unnamed. Main Street, the widest and longest street in town, and the muddiest after a rain, was the site of our business square. It consisted of four one-story buildings which housed a commissary and meat market, a post office, an ice cream parlor, and a movie house. Main Street also divided "White Town" from "Negra Town." However, the physical appearance of the two areas provided a more definite means of distinction.

The Negro citizens of Huttig were housed in rarely painted, drab red "shotgun" houses, so named because one could stand in the front yard and look straight through the front and back doors into the back yard. The Negro community was also provided with two church buildings of the same drab red exterior, although kept spotless inside by the Sisters of the church, and a two-room schoolhouse equipped with a potbellied stove that never quite succeeded in keeping it warm.

On the other side of Main Street were white bungalows, white steepled churches and a white spacious school with a big lawn. Although the relations between Negro and white were cordial, the tone of the community, as indicated by outward appearances, was of the "Old South" tradition.

As I grew up in this town, I knew I was a Negro, but I did not really understand what that meant until I was seven years old. My parents, as do most Negro parents, protected me as long as possible from the inevitable insult and humiliation that is, in the South, a part of being "colored."

I was a proud and happy child—all hair and legs, my cousin Early B. used to say—and an only child, although not blessed with the privilege of having my own way. One afternoon, shortly after my seventh birthday, my mother called me in from play.

"I'm not feeling well," she said. "You'll have to go to the market and get the meat for dinner."

I was thrilled with such an important errand. I put on one of my prettiest dresses and my mother brushed my hair. She gave me a dollar and instructions to get a pound of center-cut pork chops. I skipped happily all the way to the market.

When I entered the market, there were several white adults waiting to be served. When the butcher had finished with them, I gave him my order. More white adults entered. The butcher turned from me and took their orders. I was a little annoyed but felt since they were grownups it was all right. While he was waiting on the adults, a little white girl came in and we talked while we waited.

The butcher finished with the adults, looked down at us and asked, "What do you want, little girl?" I smiled and said, "I told you before, a pound of center-cut pork chops." He snarled, "I'm not talking to you," and again asked the white girl what she wanted. She also wanted a pound of center-cut pork chops.

"Please may I have my meat?" I said, as the little girl left. The butcher took my dollar from the counter, reached into the showcase, got a handful of fat chops and wrapped them up. Thrusting the package at me, he said, "Niggers have to wait 'til I wait on the white people. Now take your meat and get out of here!" I ran all the way home crying.

When I reached the house, my mother asked what had happened. I started pulling her toward the door, telling her what the butcher had said. I opened the meat and showed it to her. "It's fat, Mother. Let's take it back."

"Oh, Lord, I knew I shouldn't have sent her. Stop crying now, the meat isn't so bad."

"But it is. Why can't we take it back?"

"Go on out on the porch and wait for Daddy." As she turned from me, her eyes were filling with tears.

When I saw Daddy approaching, I ran to him, crying. He lifted me in his arms and smiled. "Now, what's wrong?" When I told him, his smile faded.

"And if we don't hurry, the market will be closed," I finished.

"We'll talk about it after dinner, sweetheart." I could feel his muscles tighten as he carried me into the house.

Dinner was distressingly silent. Afterward my parents went into the bedroom and talked. My mother came out and told me my father wanted to see me. I ran into the bedroom. Daddy sat there, looking at me for a long time. Several times he tried to speak, but the words just wouldn't come. I stood there, looking at him and wondering why he was acting so strangely. Finally he stood up and the words began tumbling from him. Much of what he said I did not understand. To my seven-year-old mind he explained as best he could that a Negro has no rights that a white man respected.

He dropped to his knees in front of me, placed his hands on my shoulders, and began shaking me and shouting.

"Can't you understand what I've been saying?" he demanded. "There's nothing I can do! If I went down to the market I would only cause trouble for my family."

As I looked at my daddy sitting by me with tears in his eyes, I blurted out innocently, "Daddy, are you afraid?"

He sprang to his feet in an anger I had never seen before. "Hell, no! I'm not afraid for myself, I'm not afraid to die. I could go down to that market and tear him limb from limb with my bare hands, but I'm afraid for you and your mother."

That night when I knelt to pray, instead of my usual prayers, I found myself praying that the butcher would die. After that night we never mentioned him again.

Shortly after my eighth birthday I was playing with other children on a neighbor's steps. An older boy, whom I didn't happen to like, came up and began pulling my braids. I said I was going home. The boy said, "You always act so uppity. If you knew what happened to your mother, you wouldn't act so stuck up."

"Nothing's wrong with my mother," I retorted. "I just left her."

"I'm talking about your *real* mother, the one the white man took out and killed."

"That's a story and you're a mean and nasty old boy!" I began to cry.

"It ain't. I heard my folks talking about it."

Just then the mother of one of my playmates came out on the porch and yelled at the boy. "Shut up! You talk too much. I'm going to tell your mother, and you'll get the beating of your life."

"Honey," she said to me, "don't believe nothing that nogood boy says." Still, I wondered what if he was telling me the truth?

At dinner that evening I looked intently at my parents, all the while trying to decide whether I looked like them. I could see no resemblance or likeness to myself in either of them. I remembered many little things, like the day Mother was talking to a salesman when I came in. He glanced at me, then turned to my mother.

"Have you heard from her father?" he had asked her.

When my mother said she hadn't, the salesman nodded toward me. "Does she know?"

"We haven't told her," my mother had said.

During the next few weeks I kept so much to myself that my parents decided that I must be sick. So I was "dosed" up with little pink pills. My cousin Early B. came to visit us. He was several years older than I, but I was glad to see him because he protected me from the boys who liked to taunt and tease me.

One afternoon as we walked along the millpond, I asked Early B. to tell me about my mother. He looked at me puzzled.

"Your mother?" he said guardedly, and pointed in the direction of my house. We could see her sitting on the porch.

"No. I mean my *real* mother."

"You know?"

"Yes."

"Everything?"

"Well, almost."

"Who told you? I'll knock his block off! Have you told your mamma and papa?"

"No."

We walked on in silence until we stood on the bank that divided the millpond from the town's fishing hole. Large logs floated in the water. The smell of fresh-cut lumber mixed with the odor of dead fish. As we stood there, Early B. told me of my parents.

"One night when you were a baby and your daddy was working nights at the mill, a man went to your house and told your mother that your daddy had been hurt. She rushed out leaving you alone, but she met a neighbor and asked her to listen out for you while she went to see about your daddy.

"When your daddy got home the next morning, he found you alone. He went around asking the neighbors if they had seen your mother. The neighbor your mother had asked to look after you told him what happened the night before—that she saw a man who looked like he was colored, although she didn't get a good look at him because he was walking in front of your mother.

"The news spread fast around town that your mother couldn't be found. Later in the morning, some people out fishing found her body."

Early B. stopped and sat down on the pond bank. I stood over him, looking into the dark, muddy water.

"Where did they find her?" I asked.

After a long silence Early B. pointed at the water and said, "Right down there. She was half in and half out."

"Who did it?"

"Well," he answered, "there was a lot of talk from the cooks and cleaning women who worked in 'white town' about what they had heard over there. They said that three white men did it."

"What happened to my father?"

"He was so hurt, he left you with the people who have you now, his best friends. He left town. Nobody has heard from him since."

"What did my real parents look like?"

"They were young. Your daddy was as light as a lot of white people. Your mother was very pretty—dark brown, with long black hair."

Early B.'s friends came along and he wandered off with them. I sat there looking into the dark waters, vowing that some day I would get the men who killed my mother. I did not realize that the afternoon had turned into evening and darkness had closed in around me until someone sitting beside me whispered, "It's time to go home, darling." I turned and saw my daddy sitting beside me. He reached out in the darkness and took my hand.

"How long have you known?" he asked.

"A long time," I said.

He lifted me tenderly in his arms and carried me home.

The next morning I had a high temperature. I remember the neighbors coming in, talking in quiet tones. That afternoon a playmate brought me a little box holding three guinea pigs. At first I thought they were rats. Knowing my mother's fear of rats, I hid the box in my bed.

That night the Church Sisters, who met each week at the church or at the home of some sick person to pray, gathered at our home. They knelt around my bed and prayed for my soul. I noticed the fat knees of one praying lady. It gave me an idea I couldn't resist. I eased the box to the floor and released the guinea pigs. One of them ran across the fat lady's leg. Unable to lift her weight up on the chair beside her, she lumbered around the room, screaming hysterically. The other ladies, managing to keep a few paces ahead of her, joined in the wild demonstration.

Above the hubbub I heard my mother's voice sternly demanding to know where those creatures came from. Helpless with laughter, I could not reply. The guinea pigs broke up the prayer meeting and I got my behind properly spanked. The ladies, although convinced that I certainly needed prayer, decided to do their praying for me elsewhere.

In Arkansas, even in the red clay soil of a mill town, flowers grow without any encouragement at all. Everyone's yard had some sort of flowering bush or plant all spring and summer. And in this town of Huttig, where there was so little beauty, I passionately loved all blooming things. In the woods I hunted out the first of the cowslips and spring beauties, and from open fields, the last of the Indian paintbrush. I was always bringing home bouquets.

All of the neighbors knew that the flowers in our yard were my garden, not Mother's. I had no favorites and delighted at each flower in its season. When the last roses and zinnias had died, I knew in a few short months the old lilac bush would start budding, for winter in Arkansas is short-lived. But this year was different. One morning I was out before breakfast looking for flowers to pick. All I found was a single red rose, the dew still wet on it. I can close my eyes today and see exactly how it looked. Unaccountably I turned, leaving it on its stalk, and walked into the house crying.

My mother met me at the door and I saw her face cloud with anxiety. What was the trouble? "All the other flowers were dead," I sobbed, "and my rose will die, too."

That night I heard her say to Daddy, "I can't understand that child, crying over a dying flower." Then I heard my daddy say, "Let her be. It just takes time."

My family had not spoken to me of my real mother since that day the ladies came to pray for me.

Later in the fall, on a Saturday afternoon, my father and I took a walk in the woods. It was a brisk day. Daddy thought we might find some ripe persimmons. Also, some black walnuts might have fallen from a big old tree he knew about. We walked along sniffing the air, sharp with the smell of pine needles, then came out in an open stretch in sight of the persimmon grove. I was always happy on these excursions with Daddy. I guess it was just the feeling that I couldn't be happy now, couldn't let myself be, that made me ask the question.

"Daddy, who killed my mother? Why did they kill her?"

We walked on a little way in silence. Then he pointed to some flat rocks on a slope, and we made our way there and rested. The persimmons and walnuts were forgotten. He began in tones so soft I could barely hear the words.

He told me of the timeworn lust of the white man for the Negro woman—which strikes at the heart of every Negro man in the South. I don't remember a time when this man I called my father didn't talk to me almost as if I were an adult. Even so, this was a difficult concept to explain to an eight-year-old girl; but he spoke plainly, in simple words I could understand. He wanted me to realize that my mother wouldn't have died if it hadn't been for her race—as well as her beauty, her pride, her love for my father.

"Your mother was not the kind of woman to submit," he said, "so they took her." His voice grew bitter. "They say that three white men did it. There was some talk about who they were, but no one knew for sure, and the sheriff's office did little to find out."

He said some other things about the way the Negro is treated in the South, but my mind had stopped, fastening on those three white men and what they had done. They had killed my mother.

When we walked out of the woods, my daddy looked tired and broken. He took my hand and we walked home in silence.

Dolls, games, even my once-beloved fishing, held little interest for me after that. Young as I was, strange as it may seem, my life now had a secret goal—to find the men who had done this horrible thing to my mother. So happy once, now I was like a little sapling which, after a violent storm, put out only gnarled and twisted branches.

School opened. Nothing had changed. We had the same worn-out textbooks handed down to us from the white school. With the first frosts the teacher wrestled with the potbellied stove. Days drifted by as we tried to gain an education in these surroundings. One afternoon my mother sent me to the commissary, where one could purchase anything from a nail to an automobile. Just as I reached the store, I saw some of my friends approaching. I paused on the step to wait for them. As I stood there waiting, I felt someone staring at me. I turned around and looked into the face of a rather young white man sitting on one of the benches on the porch that ran the entire length of the store. We stared at each other for a long time. I have read descriptions of the contest in staring which a bird and a snake will carry on. The two of us must have presented such a picture, although considering my own feelings, I don't know which of us symbolized the snake and which the bird.

Finally my friends called to me. I turned and entered the store with them. Once inside I looked back. The white man's eyes were still fixed on me.

People who knew my mother said I was "the living image of her." As I stood there I saw the white man's expression change from stare to puzzlement to fright. He ran his hands over his eyes as if to blot out an image. My girl friend, Beatrice, nudged me. "Daisy!" I did not move. The man jumped up from the bench and walked away, looking back at me. Beatrice asked, "What was all that? Did he say something bad to you?" I didn't answer.

As we were about to leave the store, Beatrice said, "Wait for me, I must speak to the old man." I followed her and stood back as she talked to the "old man." He was an elderly and retired mill worker who was now nearly crippled with arthritis. When the weather was clear, he always sat on the porch and chatted with the mill workers. He knew all the town's gossip. He knew all the children, both white and Negro, by name. He usually brought a lunch in a paper bag which he kept by his side. Out of this he often produced candy for us kids. Needless to say, he was to the children the most popular person in town.

I heard Beatrice tell him there was a new baby at her house. He reached in the bag and gave her a peppermint stick. He held out another for me. When I refused, he said to Bea, "What's wrong with her? She lost her sweet tooth?" Bea repeated after him, "What's the matter with you?"

I started to walk away. "Nothing," I said.

Bea caught up with me. "What's wrong with you, Daisy? You aren't any fun anymore!"

"If I want candy, I have some money to buy it," I said. "I don't want anything from white people."

The next day, after school, I asked my adopted mother if she needed anything from the commissary. No, she didn't need anything, but our neighbor wanted me to go to the store for her. I ran all the way.

As I neared the store, I saw the same young white man who had stared at me. He was seated on the same bench. I walked slowly until I reached the steps, then stopped. The man glared at me as if to say, "Look at me all you damned please." I didn't take my eyes off him. Suddenly he leaped to his feet and yelled, "Stop staring at me, you bitch!"

He started toward me. I was too frightened to move. I heard the sharp scraping sound of a chair being pushed back. I turned to see the old man standing, holding onto his chair, watching us both. The man who stared also saw him. He stopped. Then in a thin, weak voice, he muttered: "Go away! Haven't I suffered enough?" He walked slowly away.

I watched his back disappear around the corner. I was no longer afraid, for I knew he was more afraid of me than I was of him. I turned to go into the store, and the old man sank back in his chair.

During the following months I would find some way to get to the commissary at least every other day. By now I had a name for the man on the bench. "Drunken Pig." Each time he seemed a little drunker and a little dirtier than the last. At times he would stare back at me; other times he would pretend that he did not see me. But I could tell from the twitching of his mouth and his uneasy glance that he knew I was there.

One day as I was leaving the store, a little white girl about my own age, with whom I had been friends for a

long time, ran up behind me and poked me in the back.
"Daisy! Daisy!" When I turned around, she said, "Look,
Daisy, I have two pennies. Let's buy some candy and I'll
tell you about my vacation."

All my hostility and bitterness must have shown on my
face, because she pulled back with a frightened look. I
slapped her face. "Don't you ever touch me again! I don't
want your penny!"

She put her hands to her cheeks and looked at me in
disbelief. I jumped down the store steps and ran away,
tears streaming from my eyes. When I reached home, my
mother was out. I sat on the front porch, crying and
waiting for her. I wondered if I should tell my mother
and daddy what had happened. How could I ever make
my friend understand why I had struck her? I hardly
knew the reason myself.

I wanted badly to go back and tell her I was sorry, and
that I didn't really hate her. During our friendship we
had often met at the store and shared our pennies. We
would have so much fun shopping with our pennies. If
I bought winding balls, she would buy peppermint
sticks and we would divide them. How could I explain to
her that . . . Suddenly I was afraid. Suppose she went
home and told her people that I had hit her? Suppose
they came for me or my daddy that night?

I remembered hearing of a white man who went to the
home of a Negro family, carrying a wide leather belt, and
made the father beat his son to teach him to "respect
white folks." The white man's daughter was said to have
told the Negro boy, "Get off the walk, nigger, and let me
pass." The Negro boy is said to have replied, "You don't
own all the sidewalk. There's plenty of room for you to
pass, and if you think I'm going to get off the sidewalk
into the muddy street, you're crazy."

The boy did not attend school after that incident, and
the family soon moved away.

When my mother arrived home, I decided not to tell her that I had struck my white friend.

Near Christmas, the weather got very cold. The old potbellied stove at the school acted up. Most of the time we sat in class all day with our coats on. One of the boys who worked in the store in the evening with his father told us that the store had put out the Christmas toys on display. I dashed home, then hastened to the store to look at them. I rushed right past Drunken Pig. He was slumped in his usual place on the porch bench. I walked around the store looking at the toys. Three men were leaning on the counter where the dolls were. I was standing behind them, admiring the big colored doll, when the door opened and Drunken Pig came stumbling in. I heard one of the men say, "What's happened to him?"

One of the other men said, "I got an idea what's happened. You heard about that colored woman they found in the millpond a few years ago? I heard he was involved . . . leastwise, he started to drink about then, and he's been getting worse and worse ever since. He's about hit rock bottom. Too bad, 'cause he had a good job at that time."

"If he don't work, how does he buy liquor?" one of the men asked.

"He helps the bootleggers clean out their mash barrels."

I stood motionless, listening. Now that I was sure of what I had suspected, I lost all interest in the doll.

Christmas, the happy, exciting anticipation of the magic hour when Santa Claus would come laden with gifts and goodies, had no real meaning for me that year. Our church was preparing for the annual Christmas pageant, depicting the birth of the Christ Child. One of the church ladies came to see Mother to describe the part I was to play—an angel hovering over the straw crib of the Infant Jesus. "She was *so* pretty in her angel costume last Christmas," the lady cooed. Mother was smiling. She was obviously pleased. To everyone's astonishment I snapped, "*No!* I won't!"

"What is it?" Mother exclaimed. "What is it, my dear?"

"I don't want to," I cried. "I don't want no part of that play about a dead white doll!"

Mother was shocked. "I won't have that kind of talk!" she protested. "You stop that kind of talk this minute!"

"All the pictures I ever saw of Jesus were white," I screamed. "If Jesus is like the white people, I don't want any part of Him!" I fled from the room, leaving everyone in a state of consternation.

Nothing more was ever said about my appearing in the Christmas play. While my friends and family attended the Christmas pageant, I spent a lonely evening with my dog and colored doll.

With the coming of spring, I went through the daily routine of school and homework. I had come to enjoy tormenting Drunken Pig. I felt as if I were making him pay for his sin. I also blamed him for the loss of my white girl friend, whom I now missed dreadfully. I remembered how we used to meet at the store and look at magazines and daydream about places we would like to go together. One day we were looking through a magazine and saw a picture of New York, with the Statue of Liberty in the background. How would it be to go there one day, as her seventeen-year-old cousin had done? While we were musing she turned to me and asked, "Do you think it will always be like this? I can't come to your house and you can't come to mine?"

I watched Drunken Pig cringe when he was sober enough to recognize me at the commissary. He sank lower and lower. The old crippled man sitting on the porch was always the silent observer of these encounters. His eyes did not smile as much as they used to. I felt, in a

way, that he was suffering along with me and Drunken
Pig. The old man had not spoken a word to me since the
day I refused his candy.

Spring was everywhere. The trees were budding and
people were plowing their gardens. One morning I
heard Mother say to my father, "I think we should send
Daisy away for a visit with her grandmother. I don't
think this town is good for her. She doesn't take an interest
in anything around the house anymore. I asked her if she
wanted her flower garden spaded. She even refused that.
All she wants to do is go to the store. I wish I knew what
was going on in that mind of hers. I saw the mother of
that little white girl Daisy used to play with. She asked
me why her little girl and Daisy weren't friends anymore.
I didn't know what to say to her."

At that point I ran into the room and screamed, "Not
now! Please! I can't go now!"

They looked at me, puzzled. Daddy finally said, "All
right, darling, if you don't want to go to grandma's you
don't have to."

March turned damp and windy and cold, but I continued to make almost daily excursions to the commissary.
One afternoon I found Drunken Pig asleep. I came closer
and looked down at him. When he did not move, I went
into the store and bought a winding ball.

Coming out, I saw some men standing around Drunken
Pig. They were saying something to one another. After
they left I looked all around. Seeing no one but the old
man sitting dozing, a blanket around his shoulders, I
walked over to Drunken Pig and shook him lightly. When
he did not awaken, I shook him again, harder. He opened
his eyes slowly. When he saw me, he closed them again,
rubbing his hand across his face. Opening his eyes again,
he looked at me as I stood staring down at him. I don't
know how long we stayed there, staring at each other.

Finally he struggled to his feet. In a slow, pleading voice, he said, "In the name of God, leave me alone."

Then he turned, half running, half stumbling, and disappeared in the alley behind the store. I walked home happier than I had been in months; yet I was sad, for as I turned away from him, I saw my white friend standing in the door of the store watching me. I smiled and started toward her. She smiled and held out a bag that I knew held candy. I got almost to her, then turned and walked away. I suddenly remembered that she was white.

During several days of rainy weather I caught a cold and had to stay in. When my cold was better and the rains had ceased, my mother allowed me to go to the store again. At the commissary the old man was dozing in the sun. Drunken Pig wasn't around. I looked in the store. I then went next door to the post office. I came out and stood waiting. The old man sat there watching me for a while. Finally he said, "Daisy, he won't be back no more."

Hesitatingly I walked over to him. "He won't be back? Why not?"

"Because they found him in the alley this morning. That's why. He's dead."

"He can't be dead!" I argued.

"He's better off," the old man said quietly, "and so are you."

I could feel the tears come, and I started to turn away lest he see them. But then I started to sob in earnest, and I soon felt the old man's arm about me, holding me close.

"You're the only one in town to cry over that drunkard," the old man whispered in my ear.

When I stopped crying he reached into his bag and pulled out a large stick of peppermint. "I've been saving this for you," he said earnestly. "Now go home and try to forget." He loosened his embrace and I went on my way.

I walked home in a daze, clutching the candy, feeling numb all over. At home I placed the candy and the money on the table. I suddenly realized I had forgotten to make Mamma's purchase. I walked out into the yard and sat on the woodpile.

That night I kept wishing I could die. I wanted to follow Drunken Pig to hell—I was sure that was where he had gone. A few nights later, when I had gone to bed, my daddy heard me crying. He came in to comfort me. He sat on a chair next to my bed, then took my hand in his.

"I know you've been unhappy for a long time," he began. "I talked with the old crippled man who sits by the commissary. He told me about that drunk who died, and he said I should send you away. Do you want to tell me what it was about?"

Slowly between sobs I told him about my episodes with Drunken Pig. When I finished, Daddy withdrew his hand, wiped the tears from my cheeks, and told me to go to sleep and forget it. . . .

3

FROM

The Seeking

by Will Thomas

(1905–   )

A child's innocence is usually jealously guarded by his parents. It is a strange quality, at once both fragile and resilient, enduring often through the most harrowing experiences only to be shattered over a seeming trifle. That it exists only to be lost is a certainty, but its passing is always viewed with some regret. The author of this piece, Will Thomas, traded his innocence for a dawning racial consciousness one violent afternoon in Kansas City. The incident, not without humor as well as pathos, left him with this sad revelation: "When that day began, I was but a boy. At its end, I had become a Negro boy, and as such, for the first time, troubledly glimpsed walls which, like morning mists, arose between people different in something called race."

That he did not notice it earlier is not surprising since in 1917, when this incident took place, only 550,000 Negroes lived in the entire Midwest. At that time they were roughly 4 percent of the population.

Although the following selection takes place in Kansas City when Thomas was twelve, he was raised in Chicago.

He spent a good deal of his early life traveling and taking on a variety of jobs—waiter, prizefighter, journalist, and adman—before settling down to write seriously in northern Vermont.

While Thomas does pause long enough in The Seeking *to give the reader some glimpse of his childhood, the book really deals more with the author's attempt to find a place in the United States where he and his family as Negroes could live in dignity as Americans.*

. . . WHEN I was twelve we moved back to Kansas City . . . because my Uncle Bill . . . a physician, kept urging my stepfather to come there and set up practice in his office, and that is what my stepfather did.

I, of course, knowing nothing yet of such things as prejudice and segregation, was enchanted with the city of my birth. We lived in a nice house all our own. Best of all, it was right across from Spring Valley Park, a lovely four-block expanse of greenery bisected by a valley in whose center was a little lake.

During my first week, while playing in the park with Jake, a new acquaintance, he called me a bad name and I hit him. We were the same age, but Jake was taller, heavier; and I was surprised and relieved when he backed away and began crying.

"What'd you hit me for?" he whimpered. "I didn't do you nothing."

"You did so," I charged vehemently. "You called me a dirty name."

"Why, I did not, neither," he yelped indignantly. "I never even *said* no dirty word."

"Oh yes you did," I insisted, advancing warily. "Just say it again, I dare you!"

"Did you two li'l boys have any words before you fell out?"

That amused drawl came from my rear. I whirled and

there was Mike, a grin on his heavy-featured brown face, his muscular arms akimbo.

Apparently encouraged by Mike's presence, Jake suddenly ran at me, but when I pivoted to face him, he stopped abruptly, his mouth working as he wailed, "I didn't do nothin' to him and he hit me when I wasn't even lookin'!"

Mike laughed. "Well, Jakie, you're lookin' now, ain'tcha? What's a matter, you chicken?"

I glared at Mike, wishing urgently that he wouldn't egg us on, for despite my show of belligerence I quaked inwardly. I did not really like to fight.

But I had been conditioned to it in Chicago. In those first years of my life the choice was of fighting almost daily, or of becoming one of those boys whom we scornfully called "yellow" and tormented unceasingly. Worse, cowardice brought exclusion from one's gang. In preference, one fought.

Members of different gangs challenged in various ways, but the favorite and the surest way of starting hostilities was name-calling. I cannot remember that we exercised much selectivity in the choice of epithets, especially we younger kids. All were merely fighting words to which we reacted indiscriminately. A Pastelino would bristle and start swinging if taunted as a "kike," as would a Findelbaum if called a "dago" and a Donegan if jeered at as a "nigger." I would fight at any name including wop, christkiller, catlicker, harp, shine, or son-of-a-bitch.

Later, without doubt, all of us learned that those curses had personal application to various of us, but at the ages of seven to twelve we automatically struck out when *any* of those epithets were hurled at us.

And I had automatically struck tar-skinned Jake because he had called me one of those dirty names and his barefaced denial of it made his offense seem doubly heinous.

"Aw, you're talkin' crazy, li'l ole nigger," he had jeered in response to some probably fabulous brag I'd made about my former home.

And so I had hit him instantly.

And now here was Mike, who was fifteen, with the shoulders of a young bull, who wanted us to continue the fight.

"Jake called me a nigger," I explained, "so I hit him."

Jake's blubbering clipped off, his mouth dropped open, his eyes bucked. Mike was staring too, his face tightening into a ferocious scowl.

My eyes darted back and forth between the two and panic gripped me, for obviously I had in some way committed a most serious breach, but I hadn't the faintest idea of what it was.

"Well," I mumbled defensively, "he *did* call me a nigger."

"Oh he did, did he?" Mike growled, advancing slowly. I began backing away, bewildered, scared enough to wet my pants, because Mike was a "big boy," out of my class.

We were in a grassy tree-studded glade above the pretty little lake and home was a block and a half away. The ground rose sharply to our rear and so hid us from the adjacent street, making our seclusion complete, and terribly unnerving.

Mike began a bitter monologue as he followed me with short, stiff steps, his huge fists balled.

"So you think you ain't no nigger just 'cause you're lighter than somebody," he rasped. "Li'l yella nigger, you think you're cute just 'cause your father is a doctor. Just 'cause you come from Shee-caw-go. An' I'm 'ona beat th' livin'. . . ."

Jake catapulted into me then, arms flailing, and I went down, not from his wild blows, but because my feet had tangled as I tried to leap backward and sideways simultaneously.

Frantically I scrambled up only to see Mike rushing at me, right arm drawn back. My left hand shot out automatically. The impact of Mike's face against my fist jarred me to the elbow; and Mike, with a bellow, stopped for an instant and grabbed his face then hurtled at me again. I dodged and ran like a rabbit fleeing for its life.

I scurried up the hill, crashed through the hedge which bordered the park and dashed toward home; but didn't gain its sanctuary, for Mike pounded so close behind I dared not try to veer in my headlong flight when I zipped past my house.

At the far end of our block I had gained a little. I took the corner fast and gained a little more when I swerved into the alley in mid-block of that cross street. Our back gate resisted my frenzied efforts. I yanked at it, shook it, and a sore big toe later indicated I must have also kicked it. But it would not budge and the now winded Mike, jogging grimly toward me at a slow dog-trot, saw my difficulty and increased his pace alarmingly.

I abandoned the gate and leaped at the high wooden fence it conjoined. Mike thudded into it an instant later, grabbing for my feet. My frenzied lunge, when I jerked them up beyond his reach, toppled me off the fence, but happily into my own back yard. I was up and into my house via the back porch in nothing flat.

Mother, not I, discovered that in scrambling over the fence I'd ripped not only my khaki shorts but also my hide. She was alarmed and angry. How had I damaged both clothing and skin? And why was I sobbing for breath? Had I been fighting again? She had thought it would be different in Kansas City, that I wouldn't eternally be coming home with my clothes and person shredded, scaring her half to death. *Had* I been fighting?

Well, not exactly, I told her. Just sort of playing rough,

maybe, with some fellows. Gazing into her pale, troubled face I saw it was sick with concern. The impulse rose in my throat to tell her how it was—how it *really* was: how a fellow *had* to fight when called a dirty name like "nigger" or "son-of-a-bitch." And I wanted to ask her what *nigger* really meant—if it meant any different in Kansas City than it did in Chicago. Apparently it did. Maybe it meant something worse than it did in Chicago.

But I knew I mustn't, for then I would have to admit that I had been fighting, that *I* had started it; and my mother would not understand—would believe I was the real troublemaker.

Then her arms were around me, her face warm and wet against mine. Her voice broke a little when she told me that she knew I wasn't really a bad boy and she didn't mean to fuss; but that she loved me and didn't want me hurt, that she wanted me to grow up and be like my father and perhaps even follow his profession.

I hadn't thought about that for a long while, not since my year at the Art Institute when I was a little kid. My father was often in my thoughts, but remembrance of his profession had dimmed.

My father had been an artist—an oil painter, my mother reminded me. I had his name, "Will Madison Thomas," and was much like him in certain ways, only his conduct had always been gentlemanly, whereas mine— well, in that respect I was not like my father. He was not only a very talented man, but had been fine and sweet and gentle.

I did not often see my mother in tears, nor had I before felt the shudder of her sobs. Usually, it was the other way around. It was desolating. It tore me to pieces inside, and I began to cry too.

That night I did not as usual fall asleep the instant I got into bed, but lay awake for quite a while, ten minutes perhaps. I vowed to be a better boy, to behave myself, to make my mother proud by some day becoming a great painter. I would paint pictures of the lake front in Chicago, and as though it were before me, I saw the wet, rotting piles of the breakwater, its great, rusted chains; and the dank, somehow exciting smell of the backwaters was strong and real in my nostrils and the lake beyond was blue and sparkling, tossed with frothy whitecaps, and I clearly heard the thunder of the surf and how it crashed against the pilings.

Yes, from now on I *would* be a better boy. I would not worry my dear, my darling mother any more. She was a peach and I—I was just an old rotten apple core, or something worthless like that. It would not be hard to start a new leaf by sticking closer around home for a while.

Besides, Mike, or Jake, or others of that Michigan Hill gang, surely would be after me. And I knew about gangs. Maybe I'd have to duck Mike a long time, all summer perhaps. Because whether I had meant to or not I *had* hit him a good one, right in the eye.

Of course, if I happened to encounter Jake again, well, he was an ole 'fraidy cat anyway.

But Mike—

Well, I *was* going to be a better boy from now on.

Insofar as keeping close to the house was a part of the vow I'd made, I kept it. I still did not know what the neighborhood gang had against me, but evidently it was something pretty bad, for almost every time I ventured into the street boys would start at me from behind trees or rise up from the weeds of a vacant lot and chase me home.

Often, as I lolled in the safety of our front porch, Mike, one eye blackened, would slow-drag by and silently shake his fist at me and make horrible faces.

Yes, I stayed quietly at home in the interests of being

a better boy—and perhaps a whole boy—dispiritedly re-reading *The Swiss Family Robinson,* or some old favorites from my tattered set of Alger. But mainly I passed the time dreaming of the day when older and bigger, I would beat up Mike and chase him a thousand miles.

I really didn't want to stay around the house though, for on those warm days of early summer the cool, green park, so temptingly near, called to me constantly.

I don't think either my stepfather or my mother noted anything amiss. He was busy most of the time setting up his office with Uncle Bill and she was busy, too, unpacking barrels of paper-wrapped dishes, trunks, crates, buying new furniture, getting our house in order.

Most evenings she and my stepfather went out, for there were many parties, dinners and dances in their honor, since Mother was a popular hometown girl returned and her new husband, a handsome "professional" man from the elite East.

I did not much mind being alone nights, for I'd grown used to it in Chicago, nor was I afraid, or lonely to the point where it hurt inside, as so often I had been in Chicago when I was a little boy.

There were things to do; I could plunk on the piano, or fry bacon and eggs for sandwiches and go unreproved if I filled the house with smoke and smell, for I usually managed to burn everything I tried to cook. There was also a new phonograph, and I could play beloved familiars like "The Glow Worm," "Humoresque," or "Poor Butterfly" if my mood was nostalgic. There were records by a gravel-throated man named Bert Williams which were very funny. And then there were books, lots of them, neatly arranged on shelves along one living-room wall; and among these I discovered many I'd never seen which had been my father's for they contained his signature. I checked every one until I had found all with his autograph and I arranged them together on the bottom shelf.

Somehow it seemed necessary to do that when I was alone, but I did not know exactly why. I still resented my stepfather, but to please my mother I hid that feeling as best I could; and perhaps I felt that any display of interest in my real father might in some way reveal what seemed best to conceal.

Often I tried to read some of my father's books. Ruskin, Thackeray, Shakespeare, Thoreau, and such authors were beyond my comprehension. But Tennyson I read avidly, especially his *Idylls,* and was entranced by the sweetly flowing lines, even when their meaning were unclear, for to that music one could always provide meanings of his own. And I read my father's worn *Rubaiyat,* and felt blasé, believing I truly understood such lines as "The Moving Finger writes; and having writ, moves on . . ." for I *saw* that gigantic finger stirring letters into Time's sand.

But understood by me or not, I cherished those books, including the ones in German and French that had belonged to the father I never knew.

Such were some of the possibilities for filling those evenings when I was alone, although I cannot say I found them really satisfying, for often, beneath the corner street light, the neighborhood boys would gather and no matter how much I longed to, I dared not join them.

When my exile dragged into a second week I wished very much for it to end. Every day boys would straggle past our house en route to the park and threaten me in elaborate pantomime. I began to have hope, however, when they carried it to such lengths that I had to laugh, and so did they; and I thought maybe they did not hate me so much any more.

But Mike! His unforgiving glare made me squirm inside with fear; and the way he wiggled his big fist at me didn't make me feel good either.

At such times I'd stare back at him expressionlessly, but

one day I snickered, because Mike had *another* black eye, a real beaut.

My amusement died when Mike, infuriated, recklessly charged across our lawn toward our porch. I had to move briskly indeed to get inside the house before he reached me.

After that I dared only a sly grin when he passed and Mike's piggy eyes, once again red and swollen, would flame and make me quake. I thought sadly I'd probably never be a member of the gang, and wished we'd move from the neighborhood. Or, better still, that Mike would.

However, the matter was nearer resolution than I knew, for one afternoon shortly afterward a tall, slender brown boy stopped in front of our house and called, "Hiya, Willie."

I knew him. He was Jess, leader of the gang; and I suspected his friendliness was a ruse, so contented myself with a cautious, "Hi, Jess."

"Hey, how about coming on up to the park?" he invited casually.

Silently I shook my head.

"Aw, heck," Jess laughed, "nobody's gonna bother you. Come on, kid." He paused, adding in a lowered voice, "We're gonna have a rock fight with the Pecks. They're tryna run us outa the park. You game?"

Again I shook my head.

Jess climbed the terrace steps slowly, hands in hip pockets, ragged cap back on his narrow head. I hopped up from the porch swing and stood by the front door, my hand on it.

"Aw, I'm not tryna trick you, Willie," he assured me in his soft, lazy voice while his greenish-brown eyes twinkled at me. "I guess you don't trust me, hunh?"

He was right, but I dared not say so. I didn't need to, for Jess laughed and said, "Never trust nobody, kid."

He had gotten to the porch steps and to my relief he

stopped there. "Hey, you like to play in the park, don'tcha?" he asked.

"Sure."

"Well, them Pecks don't want us to, see? They think the park belongs to them. So we're gonna show 'em it don't." He paused, then chuckled. "Hey, Willie, you sure gave Mike a shiner that time. What you hit him with?"

"Why—with my fist."

"I mean," Jess said patiently, "how?" His long left arm flashed out and I jumped. He laughed and said, "Like that, maybe?"

"Why, why, yes," I admitted, wondering how he had known.

"A straight left will do it every time," he nodded approvingly. "If you was only a little heavier and your arms was a little longer, you could have cut that hunk of blubber to pieces with it."

Encouraged by his words I asked, "Who blackened his other eye?"

"Me," Jess grinned, holding up his left fist. "With this."

"Gosh," I said, awed. "Mike's a lot bigger than you."

"Ah, he ain't no trouble," Jess said negligently. He tapped his forehead with one long forefinger. "When you got it up here, Willie, you don't need so much of it here," he explained, touching his lean bicep. "So if *I* tell Mike to leave you alone, he'll do it, see? Because he knows I can knock him on his ass. So come on up to the park, Willie. We need *good* fighters today."

I hesitated, torn between the flattery and my fears.

Jess shrugged. "Willie, you're chicken," he said, starting away.

Had his tone been jeering I might have yielded to the suspicion which warned I must not go with him; but his words had been a sigh of disappointment with an overtone of surprise that I had not proved up. I ran after him.

"Hey, Jess, wait a sec. I'm—I'm coming!"

Jess paused and turning, smiled and said quietly, "I knowed you was, Willie, because I can tell when a guy is chicken, and I didn't think you was."

He dropped an arm around my shoulder and we started up the street. As I matched steps with his I felt a fierce determination to prove to Jess—and to myself—that his confidence was not misplaced.

"I just didn't want Mike beating up on me," I said breathlessly, adding, "He's a lot bigger than me."

"Aw, forget him," Jess ordered. "He ain't gonna bother you, not when I tell him not to."

And my fear of Mike died.

We walked rapidly toward the park, and when we reached the corner Jess stopped and started hurriedly loading his pockets with chunks of rock from around the base of a newly installed light pole.

We were diagonally across from the entrance to the park and I gazed in that direction warily, thinking maybe I'd see one of the Pecks peeping from behind a bush and Jess said, "Hey, Willie!" He needed to say no more, for the sharpness of his tone set me to filling my own pockets with rocks.

Jess did not enter the park at its nearest point just across the street, but strode swiftly uphill on Woodland Avenue, which flanked it. In midblock he suddenly cut over to the other side and crawled beneath a mass of heavy shrubbery, with me so close behind I could see his dusty pink soles through the holes in his shoes.

We emerged just above the glade where I'd had the trouble with Jake and Mike. When we appeared, Jess was quickly surrounded by boys who popped out of the bushes, from behind trees, and dropped down from the lushly foliaged trees themselves.

One of them breathlessly pointed downhill toward the little lake. "There's some of them Pecks, Jess. An' more sneakin' in from over by the tennis courts."

"Well, don't wet your britches," Jess said. "Them Pecks ain't no trouble."

But they were! They were big trouble. There were a lot more of them than us; and quite a few were big guys fifteen or sixteen years old, and they had plenty of rocks; and, worse, some had air rifles.

It was my first glimpse of the Pecks and it stirred within me the same dread thrill soldiers must experience when first the enemy is sighted.

I remember wondering why the gang below was known as "The Pecks," but that trifling matter swept from my mind when Jess eased up from behind the bush where he had been studying the foe, grimly hefting a rock, shaking it around in his hand getting the feel of it.

There were perhaps eighteen of us, mostly shabbily dressed boys in our early teens. Our eyes were pinned on Jess; we imitated his venomous snarl and took courage from him because he was our leader, Chief of the Michigan Hill Gang.

I didn't know I'd been holding my breath until Jess seemed to coil and uncoil in one fluid motion before the rock whizzed from his hand. My heart leaped when in the center of the rival gang a husky blond youth reeled back, clutching his head. Jess's long throw had scored.

The members of the other gang froze, stared numbly at the boy who had been hit or fearfully gaped up to where we still remained hidden.

Then Jess threw again, scored another hit, and yelled, "Lettum have it, men!"

We did, furiously, wildly, whizzing a hail of stones down on the foe who broke and ran. Jess plunged downhill with a harsh, jubilant cry, and we poured after him, screaming, charging in for the kill.

The big blond boy, victim of Jess's unerring aim, blood trickling from a cut cheek, ran toward us rather than away. A few of his followers hesitated, then edged after him, and began returning our fire with stones of their own.

Jess raced straight toward the blond boy. Unable to check his speed on the slippery grass, he ran right into the boy's powerful swing and went down.

Even as he hit the ground and began rolling away from the blond boy's vicious kicks, Mike smashed into the enemy leader at knee level and flattened him.

Meanwhile, encouraged by their leader's prowess in felling ours, some of the Pecks swarmed back.

Despite my size and age, I was no amateur at this type of combat and I moved about cagily, circling to protect my rear, fending a wild thrust here, ducking a ferocious swing there, getting in a lick of my own when I could.

It became quickly evident that we had made a tactical error in attacking so impulsively, for we found ourselves almost surrounded as more and more Pecks joined the fray with wild whoops.

Jess, again on his feet, realized the situation, and even as a foe tumbled down from his blow, he yelled for a retreat—an order that some of our boys had not awaited. The rest of us rallied behind Jess, backing up the hill from which we had attacked. We would have been over-whelmed except for the restraining effect of Jess's deadly fire upon our pursuers.

But the blond boy wasn't deterred by it. He burst ahead and swung at Jess. This time, Jess had firm footing and he leaned away from the blow and I heard the *splat* his fist made against the blond boy's face. The boy staggered back, pawing wildly, trying to keep from going down. But he did go down and when he tried to get up he couldn't and we took advantage of the ensuing brief, shocked lull to further retreat.

We ran uphill, across our glade, through the thick, bushy hedge which marked the park boundary, and when we hit the street we were fairly flying. Most of our gang slashed through the tall weeds of the big vacant lot on the corner and kept going despite Jess's yells for them to stop.

I was right beside Jess and although I also wanted to keep going I stopped when he did and dropped down beside him in the weeds.

Mike, his thick chest heaving, dirty, sweaty face fiercely contorted, was the only other who stuck with Jess and we three lay flat on our bellies, peeking toward the park, waiting to see if the Pecks would follow us.

When they appeared, a shrieking pack of triumphant young savages with shirt-tails flying wildly, they jumped and danced and jeered, screaming invitations for us to return and fight again.

It was then I began to distinguish words, phrases, in the jumbled din the enemy was making, such as "goddamn black sonsabitches," "scary-cat nigger bastards," but above all else a shrilling chorus of "nigger-nigger-nigger-nigger."

Someone must have summoned the police, for a patrol car came clanging up the street. Jess said softly, "Uh uh!" The Pecks broke and ran and we lay as still as death among the weeds.

The police lumbered into the park after the Pecks, but soon returned, red and sweating, and after looking up and down the street, climbed back into their car and departed.

Jess released a whistling breath, stood up and said, "Come on, men, let's get out of here."

We went, a disheveled trio, defeated but not downcast, our faces cut and lumpy, Jess in the middle, Mike and I flanking him. There was a swagger in our unhurried pace, a defiant set to our shoulders.

"Next time," Jess said, thinking aloud, "we gotta have more men. I didn't think them Pecks would have so many." He chuckled and gave Mike a hard shove. "Man, you sure knocked the taste outa that big yella-haired Peck."

Mike clumsily caught his balance and his wide grin showed how pleased he was by Jess's praise. "Well, you touched him up lightly and po-litely yourself," he replied, "an'," he added, patting my shoulder, "this here li'l ole yella nigger didn't do so bad, neither."

A flush of pleasure warmed me and I knew I should let well enough alone and I meant to, but the words came out anyhow and they were, "Don't go calling me any dirty names, Mike."

Mike stopped, hands on hips, his grin fading into an angry glower. "Who called you a dirty name?" he demanded. "Are you crazy? Here I try to say something good about you and you—you. . . ." He took a step toward me, fists balled, and I backed away. Jess stepped between us and shoved Mike back.

"What dirty name you talkin' about, Willie?" Jess asked, regarding me curiously.

"Well, he called me a *nigger*," I said, trying for truculence and managing only a low mumble.

"Well, if you ain't a nigger, what are you?" Jess didn't sound angry at all, just puzzled.

Mike tried to edge around Jess to get at me, but Jess said casually, "Let him alone, Mike," and Mike stopped, but he was almost doing a jig of rage, and tears started at the corner of his eyes. His mouth shot out and he looked like a balloon on the verge of bursting.

"Looka here, Willie," Jess said quietly, "how come you don't like to be called 'nigger'? You don't think you are a Peck, do you?"

"Yah, he thinks he's a Peck," Mike yelped, half crying. "Thinks because he's light he's better'n us. I—"

"Shut up, Mike," Jess ordered gruffly. "Well, what about it, Willie?"

"Well," I said, fumbling to explain what I did not understand, "it is a bad word. You fight a guy that calls it to you."

"You fight a *white* guy that calls you that," Jess corrected. "You fight a Peck when he calls you that or 'darky' or 'coon' or 'Sambo' or 'snowball.'"

A dim light was dawning, a foggy understanding. I said, "Those guys we were fighting—they were all white? Is that why you call them Pecks?"

"Well, gah-ah-ah-dam!" Mike exclaimed unbelievingly. "You tryna say you don't know what a Peck is—a Peckerwood? Where you been all your life, man?"

"Why—why, in Chicago," I said bewilderedly.

Jess laughed. "Hey, Willie, didn't you sure 'nough know what a Peck was?"

"I thought it was the name of a gang," I confessed, ashamed of what now seemed colossal ignorance, "like in Chicago. We called our gang the 'Dearborn Street Sluggers,' because we lived on Dearborn Street. But mostly we just called ourselves 'The Dearborns.' So when you said we were going to fight the Pecks, I just thought—"

Jess laughed. Mike whistled as though amazed. Jess dropped an arm around my shoulders and said, "Willie, you got a lot to learn." I tried to hold back the tears, but they came and I began to blubber and Mike gave me a punch in the back, not hard, and said, "Well, it ain't nothing to cry about, Willie."

It was a good moment, but also one of confusion about many matters still unclear. I gulped and scrubbed away my tears and Jess and Mike sat down on the curbing, with me between them, and Jess put his arm around me again and gave me a squeeze and said gruffly, "Everything's all right, Willie," and Mike said wonderingly. "So *that's* how come you popped Jake that day in the park! I'll be doggoned. You *sure* got a lot to learn boy."

I began learning right then, and when my instructors had finished that day's lesson, I knew that I should not hit a member of "our race," or even resent his calling me a "nigger" or the like, for it was just a kidding way we had of using a hated word.

But it still was not at all clear.

I learned many new, complex, and perplexing rules that morning, among which were: that because my skin was fair I must not refer to darker boys by *their* color, must not give reason to make them think I thought myself better because of my lightness. And that just because my stepfather was a doctor, I'd better not act like that made me any better than the other boys. Because packing-house laborers, Pullman porters, cooks and maids and porters were just as good as anybody, including doctors.

Mike thawed completely during that strange session when I was initiated into the society to which I had not known I belonged, for I had not known it even existed: The Dark Brotherhood.

When that day began, I was but a boy. At its end I had become a *Negro* boy, and as such, for the first time, troubledly glimpsed walls which, like morning mists, arose between people different in something called race.

In the end I still could not grasp all that, and all I *knew* was that I really hadn't thought myself better because my stepfather was a doctor, and certainly not because my skin was fairer than that of most of my new playmates; for I had not given a thought to my looks until then, except back in those tormented days when my mother had made me wear my hair in curls.

I also knew that the word *nigger* was not, as I had always thought, just one of the bad words which could be used indiscriminately. Even so I was still confused about it because it was all right for colored people to use it in reference to one another, yet it was wrong when white people used it in speaking to, or about us. But we did not use that word in reference to them, or to them even when we cursed them to their faces.

4

FROM

Let Me Live

by Angelo Herndon

(1913–   )

This short episode took place in Wyoming, Ohio, the town where Angelo Herndon was born. It is illustrative of the numbing shock and pain that accompany a Negro child's recognition of his "otherness." It is a commonplace to say that children, with their forthright candor, can be very cruel, but the irrational element of racial bigotry here turns a typical childhood incident into a deep, long-lasting hurt. Also of interest in this selection is the way the Negro's unfounded sense of guilt is passed from generation to generation.

Angelo Herndon became a cause célèbre when he was arrested in Atlanta in 1932 at the age of nineteen. He was charged with attempting to incite insurrection after he led a demonstration of unemployed white and Negro workers demanding relief. His conviction in a Georgia court was overturned by the United States Supreme Court in 1937.

In addition to writing Let Me Live, *Herndon edited* The Negro Quarterly, *a short-lived journal which pur-*

eflect the "true aspiration of the Negro people
ir tradition of struggle for freedom."

ONE day I saw white children at a game of marbles.
Innocent of any evil thought or expectations, I joined their
game. As my misfortune would have it, I shot all their
marbles out of the ring. A white boy, livid with rage,
called me a "nigger." "Nigger?" I repeated, not understanding. "What does 'nigger' mean?" The boys burst out
laughing and I laughed with them good-naturedly. But
the incident hereupon went beyond name-calling.

"Do you want to know what 'nigger' means?" asked the
white boy spitefully. "Let me show you."

Together with the other boys he began to pelt me with
stones and I fled for dear life. After a while, tiring of their
sport, they let me alone. With feelings smarting more
than did the bruises on my body, I ran to my mother,
weeping. Between my sobs, I managed to gasp the all-
important question:

"Mother, what does 'nigger' mean?"

A look of pain and indignation came into her face. She
wanted to know who had used that nasty word to me.
When I had explained, she put on the sing-song voice
that she always used whenever she read out the Scrip-
tures. She intoned the following verse from the Song of
Songs:

"Look not at me so because I am black for the sun
hath burned me, the children of my father were angry
with me and they made me watchman of their vineyard,
but my own vineyard I have not kept."

She went on to explain to me that because we Negroes
sinned against God, against His only begotten Son, and
the Holy Ghost, therefore He has humbled us in our
pride and vanity; He has made slaves of us for the white
man to oppress and to mistreat, so that we might learn to
be obedient and to walk in His way, and sin no more.

Moved by her own words, she raised her beautiful voice in song as was her way when religion came upon her:

> *You can't hide, sinner, you can't hide!*
> *Oh, tell me what you going to do?*
> *You can't hide!*
> *When the mountains start falling, you can't hide!*
> *You can't hide, sinner, you can't hide!*

As I listened to her, a deep sense of guilt came over me. To be sure, I must be a sinner too, and the fact that the white boys called me "nigger" must have been the will of God. Already I felt as if by this act alone, by being humiliated in spirit and bruised in body, that I was expiating for the pride and the vanity which my mother charged against our race. . . .

5

FROM

Dark Symphony

by Elizabeth Adams

(1910?-   )

When a child is hurt either physically or emotionally by someone outside his family, he will, in all likelihood, turn to his parents for aid and comfort. This is true for children of any race, but the problem takes on added significance if the child is black. While all parents have the option of advising the child to follow the adage "an eye for an eye," or admonishing him to "forgive and forget," it is only the white child who can seek revenge with impunity. If the Negro child retaliates, he risks incurring the wrath of the entire white community.

Elizabeth Adams' parents had faith in the course of nonviolence. It is the harder of the two courses for a child to understand, and certainly the more frustrating, but Elizabeth finally came to believe her mother's words: "A lady never strikes back."

Miss Adams was born a Protestant about 1910 in Santa Barbara, California. After graduating from high school she converted to Catholicism and hoped to enter a convent. The Depression thwarted her plans, however, and she turned her talents toward a literary and dramatic career.

In the following selection she tells of her early school days in California.

ONE day a stranger arrived at school. We called her the "new girl" because we had never seen her before. When Mary asked her to join our game she shook her head and refused. Pointing in my direction she declared: "I won't play with her because—*she's a nigger.*"

That was the first time that I had ever heard—the word.

I was a very small child when this happened, but I can remember the queer expressions that passed over the countenances of my playmates. A few backed away, a frightened look in their eyes. Others gazed at me—then at one another.

I think every Colored person in the world can recall the first time he or she was called by this uncomplimentary title. Countee Cullen, Negro poet, wrote a poem about it. He called the poem INCIDENT. The poet says:

Once riding in old Baltimore
    Heart-filled, head-filled with glee,
I saw a Baltimorean
    Keep looking straight at me.

Now I was eight and very small,
    And he was no whit bigger,
And so I smiled, but he poked out
    His tongue, and called me, 'Nigger.'

I saw the whole of Baltimore
    From May until December;
Of all the things that happened there
    That's all that I remember.

In my case I wondered what had happened to change me so unexpectedly that my playmates would stare wild-eyed.

Mary Carty patted my hand and said, "Never mind, Elizabeth. I love you."

After school hours I marched home (yes, I say *marched*, because I usually hummed something like a tune to step to) and ran into the house and asked:

"Mamma, what am I?"

Mother was busy and replied nonchalantly. "You're Mamma's little girl."

I shook my head. This was the wrong answer.

She then informed me that I was Mamma's and Papa's little girl if it would make me any happier to have both parents included.

I shook my head again.

I asked: "Mamma—what's a 'nigger'?"

My mother was very tactful. She inquired first where I had heard the word. I told her. She suggested that we have a "little talk": and so we went into an adjoining room.

I remember that Mamma became very busy with her sewing as she began the conversation. She kept biting off bits of thread and seemed unable to find the eye in the needle. She told me that the word "nigger" was not a "nice" word. It was not complimentary. Next she hastened to add that perhaps the little white girl who called me that did not know any better. Then followed the admonition to love the little girl just the same, even though she refused to join a game in which I was playing.

Yes, Mamma wanted me to think kindly of her. No matter how many times she called me "nigger" I was not to strike her, it seemed.

"I do not want you to strike her," my mother said. "It is not that she is better than you that I ask this; but you must not strike at people. A lady never strikes back."

Then I was told that if any difficulties came up I was to tell mother; and she would see my school teacher. She next requested that I reveal the little girl's name. It was Lillian. How could I forget, when it involved so much explanation!

That night when I said my prayers before retiring, Mother demanded that I ask God to "bless Lillian." I did so because I had to obey. Of my own volition I would not have bothered to have told God anything about her. I did not hate the child. I was rather dazed over the affair; because for the first time the fact that my skin was dark had been brought to my attention. I had thought of myself as "Elizabeth" because my parents said that was my name. Mary Carty was "Mary Carty" because she said that was her name. I had never thought of her being different in color to myself.

"Don't worry about it any more," Mamma said as she tucked me in bed that night.

Of course I had no intention of worrying. I did not know what it meant to worry. After I had asked God to bless my parents, grandparents, my school teacher and everybody else far and near including my dolls and "Rags" (the pet who slept in a dog-house out in the back yard) there was nothing else to do but go to sleep. . . .

The awakening of race consciousness wrought a series of bewildering revelations in my life.

I discovered (to my surprise) that Lillian's contempt for dark people influenced several playmates, which resulted in my loss of their friendship. Nevertheless, there were other white children who (like little Mary Carty) remained ever faithful and tried to amend the wrongs of the easily-persuaded-to-become-prejudiced of their own group by engaging in fierce word-battles with them; and who imparted to Colored children petty ways and means of revenge. Thus it was that while my mother saw to it that I implored the Omnipotent to bless Lillian, Mary Carty conscientiously instructed me as to the proper procedure of turning up one's nose at an enemy.

"Doncha be scared a-her," Mary consoled whenever we talked of Lillian. "I'm with you!"

Hence there were mornings when we two (silhouettes in black and white) strutted hand-in-hand past my adversary. And Mary (to whom had been bequeathed an aquiline nose by right of inheritance from Anglo-Saxon ancestors) sniffed and turned up her nose as a gesture of indignation. I tried to imitate her. But alas, I (to whom had been bequeathed a short, stubby, button-like covering for the anterior part of the nasal fossae by right of inheritance from African ancestors) could only sniff disdainfully—my nose (being not of stream-line design) proved a blunt weapon in snooty combat. But I sniffed. I could not strike Lillian without having upon my conscience the guilt of disobedience to my parents. But I could sniff.

It worried my little white companion considerably that my nose (unlike hers) could not be upturned. She was puzzled. So was I. But there was nothing we could do about it. So after numerous disheartening lessons, Mary, exasperated, lost hope and ceased coaching.

"You'll just be happy sniffin' at everybody what makes you mad," she concluded.

Unfortunately, Lillian addressed a few of the other Colored children by the word and they made plans for her to be torn limb from limb. Then extremely troublesome times ensued for me when the dark group *demanded* that I join their ranks.

"We're goin' to beat her up!" they informed me.

The idea astounded and stunned. Helplessly I sought to evade the issue.

"I can't fight," I told the ring-leader, a very pretty

Colored child with the face of a cherub and the fists of a Goliath.

"Why not?" she wanted to know.

"Because my mother says I can't. My father says I can't," I replied.

"Beat her up and don't tell them," she suggested.

Fully awakened to the realization that the word was specially devised to carry degrading implications, a conflict began within. If being called "nigger" was supposed to make a person fight, then I wanted to fight. But my hands were tied by the invisible cords of obedience: for my parents having told me that all things done in secret would be witnessed by God, I imagined the Deity peering down at me through the fleecy clouds; and presumed there was some secret method of direct communication between God and my elders so that He could let them know at once if I disobeyed.

The ring-leader threatened to "beat me up" if I failed to comply with her wishes.

That night when I began the recitation of bed-time prayers I decided not to mention Lillian. This white child was a burden on my soul. So I avoided asking that she be showered with toys and made a good girl.

My mother, noticing the omission, demanded a repetition of the prayers. Repeated they were. But again she heard no audible plea for Lillian's share of blessings. Then in no uncertain terms Mother commanded that I incorporate in my heavenly petitions the name of this child who humiliated me. Reluctantly I acquiesced.

Every night my mother led the forgive-thine-enemy campaign.

Once or twice I wondered how God would like it if someone called Him "nigger"; then remembered that according to my Sunday-school teacher no one dared to question or wonder about the Creator.

Finally, owing to Mother's blessed patience, I ceased

battling. Of my own volition I asked the Great Unseen Giver of Gifts to give my enemy bountiful treasures from His storehouse of supplies.

I now look back on this part of my life with mingled emotions—mostly smiles. Whenever there is reason to refer to it in the presence of Caucasian friends someone invariably asks with solemn hesitant voice:

"Isn't it difficult for a Colored child to be really happy after finding out that he or she is a victim of racial prejudice for life?"

But in fact the child-victim of racial prejudice, though shocked on becoming aware of the disreputable intention of the word "nigger," regards it merely as a strange happening, a baffling mystery and in time something to fight over; he is too young to have the slightest perception of the many complexities that make up the problem of Negro life.

I particularly recall how my curiosity became aroused as I began to notice the racial differences in my schoolmates. Some were white, red, yellow, brown, black. There were marked distinctions in features and texture of hair. Wondering about these things led me to seek knowledge from the oracle of oracles—Mother.

How did it happen, I wanted to know, that I was born Colored instead of Chinese, Indian or another race? Why had I not been given stringy, taffy-yellow hair like Mary Carty's? Why were my eyes brown instead of blue? Why did I have round eyes instead of slant ones like Kim, my little Japanese playmate? Why? Why? Why? Oh, yes: why was I born anyway? Where had I come from? Where did everybody come from?

Mother volunteered information: and that was how I first heard of the stork.

"An' th' stork brought me as a present to you and Papa?" I queried.

"That's right," Mother responded.

"An' flew right over our house an' dropped me down the *chimmbly?*"

"That's what I have just said," remarked Mother-Oracle. "But the word is chimney, dear, chimney."

The stork-story held me spell-bound. With the vivid imagination with which the majority of normal children are endowed, I visualized the white bird circling over our housetop. According to Mother I slumbered peacefully in a large black satchel which the Bird of Travel held securely in his bill. Then he placed satchel and me right into a cradle.

The idea fascinated me. But if my Mother thought the telling of the story thus far would suffice she was mistaken. My mind was a bit hazy concerning a few items which I considered important.

"Where did the stork get me?" I asked.

"From heaven," remarked Mother with an air of intense conviction. "There are trillions, billions and millions of little babies there," she went on as though answering my thought. "And God, being busy, sends them to earth by the stork."

She next proceeded to describe the sales-tag on the satchel in which I reclined, saying that it read:

Please Deliver To—
> Mr. and Mrs. Daniel Henderson Adams,
> Santa Barbara, California
> One baby-girl to be named,
>> Elizabeth Laura.

"Why didn't the stork leave me at Mary Carty's house or Kim's house instead of giving me to you and Papa?" I demanded suspiciously.

Ah—that was a brain wrecker for Mother! All she had to do was to explain to me in simplified language why I, a Colored child, had not been presented as a gift of joy to our white neighbors, the Carty's, or to Kim's family, our Japanese neighbors.

Mother coughed a couple of times and then continued.

"The stork is very wise," she said in a low voice as though sharing a secret. "He has a wonderful eye for color. Likes to see everything match. So he gives white babies to white mothers and fathers and red babies to red mothers and fathers and so on and so on until all the different colors of parents have babies to match. Isn't that wonderful?"

I mused. Smiled. Grinned. Yes, it was wonderful! That explained everything—why Mary Carty was white, Kim Japanese, and I Colored. God had painted us different colors—then the stork selected us to blend harmoniously with the bodily color-scheme of our respective families.

I was almost convinced when one other thought popped into my mind.

"But," I faltered, "how does the stork know Mammas and Papas want the babies?"

Mother cleared her throat and coughed again.

"They pray to God, asking Him for their children," she said. "Then He orders the stork to deliver them to earth."

Then with the dramatic air of an actress, Mother leaned back in her chair and a sad, sad look crept into her eyes.

"All children should love their parents, dear," she sighed. "For they have to work hard, save their money and have a nice home all ready for the little baby when it arrives. And the poor stork," she said pathetically, "goes from house to house, country to country—all over the world. As soon as he delivers one baby he has to fly right back to heaven for another to take to some other family."

That explanation settled all doubts. I needed to hear no more. My sympathy rested with the stork. I pictured the poor bird weary and hungry—his wings rain-drenched one day and scorched and sagging from the heat of the sun on a bright day.

I threw my arms around my mother's neck: glad, glad indeed, that the over-worked bird had remained constant in his fidelity to duties of transportation and had not collapsed from exhaustion while en route to our house.

Even as a very small child I believed that good news and the meritorious achievements of others should be shared, that was why I started for the door to pass the word along to Mary Carty and Kim.

"Where are you going?" Mother demanded.

When I told her she caught me quickly and set me down.

"Now listen," she said positively. "You must never, never tell others the story about the stork. It's our secret!"

A secret! I looked at her.

"Maybe—maybe Mary an' Kim don' know about the stork," I murmured regretfully as my mother's restraining hand continued to rest upon my shoulder, and indications of my opportunity to be a publicity-agent for the stork began to fade.

"Their mothers will tell them," came the response. "Listen, dear—" Mother's tone softened. I looked at her and she whispered:

"We must keep this a family secret. The stork wants all families to keep the story of his coming to themselves. He wants to surprise everybody."

Surprise! I understood that word. A surprise meant something one did not expect and it always brought happiness (so I believed)—unexpected happiness such as rice pudding for dinner, a new doll, a new dress.

I had one more request to make.

"What now?" Mother inquired.

I whispered loudly:

"May I tell Papa when he comes home?"

A few weeks later, there stood in my mother's room a dainty basket-shaped bed decorated with pretty blue and white ribbons, and in it was a baby. A real, live baby!

"It's your Baby-Brother," the lady in the white uniform told me.

I did not like the lady in the white uniform. She was Colored, but even that did not make us congenial. I thought her impatient and very, very cross when she slapped my fingers as I slyly started to poke them into Baby-Brother's eyes to see if he would squeal. Another grievance held against her was that she would not let me see Mother until late in the afternoon, and then for only a short time. And she always spoiled my visits by beginning to speak as soon as I crossed the threshold of Mother's room, saying: "*We* haven't long to stay, Mother. *We* must hurry along."

I did not like the idea of her calling my mother, "Mother"—and I did want to stay a long time in Mother's room. I wondered: what right did she have anyway, trying to talk for both of us?

Then something strange happened about the third day after I first saw Baby-Brother. I went over to the fireplace. No fire burned, and no one was looking. I tried to catch a glimpse of the stork.

Alas! Only the black, sooty channel of the chimney was visible.

I sought the lady in the white uniform, knowing that Mother-Oracle was not available.

"Where's the stork?" I asked.

She snapped at me.

"Stork? What are you talking about?"

"The stork that brought Baby-Brother!"

"Questions! Questions! Don't you ever think of anything else but questions?" she snapped again.

"Please, ma'am," I persisted. "Where is he?"

"He's flown!" she said and walked out of the room.

And though it is true that I disliked the lady in the white uniform (and seldom had one confidence in a

believed-to-be-enemy) nevertheless Baby-Brother's existence being a visible sign of the stork's arrival—could I do
aught else but believe she spoke the truth?

II

THE NINETEENTH CENTURY:

A Time of Upheaval

IT is extremely difficult, if not impossible, to understand life
as it was in this country a little more than a century ago. If
slavery, the "peculiar institution," did not exactly flourish, it
most certainly existed, with all its unbelievable cruelty. By
1860 there were nearly 3,000,000 slaves in the South, but,
contrary to belief, slave ownership was not widespread. Probably not more than 400,000 of the 8,000,000 Southern whites
in that year were slaveholders. In addition, there was a class
of Negroes freed by their owners for one motive or another.
They made up about 10 percent of the Negro population in
the South.

Children of slaves had a most unnatural childhood. More
often than not they did not know where or when they were
born, or who their parents were since they were frequently
separated from them at a very early age. It is interesting to
reflect upon the fact that in many cases the father was the
white plantation master. (It was, as a matter of fact, in his
interest to have as many children as possible by his female

slaves since the issue was regarded as additional property.)
How did he feel to see his black child brutally whipped,
perhaps by one of his legitimate white children? Did he feel
any remorse? Or did he just regard the child as he would a
piece of inanimate property?

Slave children were, of course, forbidden an education.
Their function in that society was to serve. They were beaten
if they deviated from their expected conduct in any way.
Some were fortunate enough to escape to free states. Most did
not.

Before the Civil War the number of Negroes in the South
climbed steadily. After the war, however, while many chose
to remain on their former plantations on a sharecrop basis,
others fled the South, and the decades following the 1860's
show a gradual decline in the percentage of Negroes in the
total population of the South.

Children were still pressed into service, but this time by
their families. Schools were opened for Negro children and
the education of a race began. The twentieth century loomed
ahead.

1

Memoirs of a Monticello Slave:

The Life of Isaac Jefferson

As dictated to Charles Campbell
in the 1840's by Isaac,
one of Thomas Jefferson's slaves

(1775–1850?)

*Isaac Jefferson was born into slavery at Monticello in
December, 1775. The country was in arms against England, and Isaac's earliest memories go back to the days
when Thomas Jefferson was governor of Virginia, and
the British captured Richmond in 1781. Isaac was taken
to Yorktown as a prisoner of the British, but was released
at the end of the war, at which time he returned to
Monticello. When Jefferson went to Philadelphia in 1790
as Secretary of State (not as President, as Isaac mistakenly
recalls) he took the fifteen-year-old slave with him. After
Jefferson resigned in 1793, both Jefferson and Isaac returned to Monticello where Isaac remained for nine years.
For the next quarter century he lived with Jefferson's
son-in-law, Thomas Mann Randolph. He came back to
nurse the ex-President in his old age, and after Jefferson
died, spent the last years of his life in Petersburg where
Charles Campbell, editor, scholar, and author, came to*

know him and record these reminiscences in the 1840's.

It is not often that we see a master from the viewpoint of a slave—particularly a master of such national and international prominence. Thomas Jefferson may have been a reluctant slaveholder, but he was a slaveholder, nevertheless. By 1774 he owned 50 slaves of his own, in addition to 135 whom he held on behalf of his wife. After the Revolution this number increased to over 200. He was a benevolent master. He tried to keep families together even when he bought or sold slaves, or when he accepted or gave them in payment of debt. He maintained his landholdings by slave labor throughout his adult life.

Yet Thomas Jefferson, as paradoxical as it may seem, found slavery an abhorrent institution. As early as 1776 he favored and proposed abolition of the slave trade, and in his famous Notes on Virginia, *he admitted that slavery was a cruel institution that destroyed the morals of the masters while degrading the slaves. Freedom, he avowed, was a gift of God, and men had no right to take it away. (Nevertheless, at no time did he consider freeing his own slaves, partially because of the hostile attitude of Virginians toward freedmen at this time, and partially because it would have meant complete economic ruin for him personally.)*

The Notes *did provide for the gradual emancipation of slaves. Jefferson suggested that slaves born after a certain date should be freed, trained at public expense for useful employment, and then sent away to a colony either abroad, or further West on the American continent, at which time white settlers would be imported from Europe to replace them. Never did Jefferson contemplate a society where black and white would live side by side. He was nearing the end of his life when he summed up his thoughts by asserting, "Nothing is more certainly written in the book of fate than that these people are to be free. Nor is it less certain that the two races, equally free, can-*

not live in the same government." But even the idea of emancipation was radical enough in 1781 for Jefferson to withhold publication of his Notes *on Virginia. As he himself put it, "The public mind would not bear the proposition."*

In the following selection, Isaac Jefferson recalls his life at Monticello in the late eighteenth century as a slave of the man who insisted that slavery was a "great political and moral evil."

LIFE OF ISAAC JEFFERSON OF PETERSBURG, VIRGINIA, BLACKSMITH, containing a full and faithful account of MONTICELLO & the FAMILY there, with notices of many of the distinguished CHARACTERS that visited there, with his REVOLUTIONARY experience & travels, adventures, observations & opinions, the whole taken down from his own words.

CHAPTER 1

Isaac Jefferson was born at Monticello: his mother was named Usler (Ursula) but nicknamed Queen, because her husband was named George & commonly called King George. She was pastry-cook & washerwoman: Stayed in the laundry. Isaac toated wood for her: made fire & so on. Mrs. Jefferson would come out there with a cookery book in her hand & read out of it to Isaac's mother how to make cakes tarts & so on.

Mrs. Jefferson was named Patsy Wayles,[1] but when Mr. Jefferson married her she was the widow Skelton, widow of Batter (Bathurst) Skelton. Isaac was one year's

---

[1] Martha, youngest daughter of John Wayles, a native of Lancaster, England, a lawyer, who lived at "the Forest" in Charles City county, Va. He was married three times & dying in May 1773 left three daughters one of whom married Francis Eppes, (Father of John W. Eppes who married Maria daughter of Thomas Jefferson) & the other Fulwar Skipwith. Mr. Jefferson inherited the Shadwell & Monticello estates. The portion that he acquired by marriage was encumbered with a (British) debt & resulted in a heavy loss. Martha Skelton was 23 years old in 1772 when She married Mr. Jefferson.

child with Patsy Jefferson: she was suckled part of the time by Isaac's mother. Patsy married Thomas Mann Randolph.[2] Mr. Jefferson bought Isaac's mother from Col. Wm Fleming of Goochland. Isaac remembers John Nelson an Englishman at work at Monticello: he was an inside worker, a finisher. The blacksmith was Billy Ore; (Orr?) the carriage-maker Davy Watson: he worked also for Col. Carter of Blenheim, eight miles from Monticello. Monticello-house was pulled down in part & built up again some six or seven times. One time it was struck by lightning. It had a Franklin rod at one eend. Old master used to say, "If it hadn't been for that Franklin the whole house would have gone." They was forty years at work upon that house before Mr. Jefferson stopped building.

CHAPTER 2

Mr. Jefferson came down to Williamsburg in a phaeton made by Davy Watson. Billy Ore did the iron-work.[3] That phaeton was sent to London & the springs &c was gilded. This was when Mr. Jefferson was in Paris. Isaac remembers coming down to Williamsburg in a wagon at the time Mr. Jefferson was Governor. He came down in the phaeton: his family with him in a coach & four. Bob Hemings drove the phaeton: Jim Hemings was a body-servant: Martin Hemings—the butler. These three were brothers: Mary Hemings & Sally, their Sisters. Jim & Bob bright mulatoes, Martin, darker. Jim & Martin rode on horseback. Bob went afterwards to live with old Dr. Strauss in Richmond & unfortunately had his hand shot off with a blunderbuss. Mary Hemings rode in the wagon. Sally Hemings' mother Betty was a bright mulatto

---

[2] Sometime Governor of Virginia.

[3] Capt. Bacon says: John Hemings made most of the wood-work & Joe Fosset made the iron-work.

woman & Sally mighty near white: She was the youngest
child. Folks said that these Hemings'es was old Mr.
Wayles' children. Sally was very handsome: long straight
hair down her back. She was about eleven years old when
Mr. Jefferson took her to France to wait on Miss Polly.
She & Sally went out to France a year after Mr. Jefferson
went. Patsy went with him at first, but she carried no
maid with her. Harriet one of Sally's daughters was very
handsome. Sally had a son named Madison, who learned
to be a great fiddler. He has been in Petersburg twice:
was here when the balloon went up—the balloon that
Beverly sent off.

Mr. Jefferson drove faster in the phaeton than the
wagon. When the wagon reached Williamsburg Mr.
Jefferson was living in the College (of Wm. & Mary)
Isaac & the rest of the servants stayed in the Assembly-
house—a long wooden building. Lord Botetourt's picture
(statue) was there. The Assembly-house had a gallery
on top running round to the College. There was a well
there then: none there now. Some white people was living in one end of the house: a man named Douglas was
there: they called him Parson Douglas.[4] Mr. Jefferson's
room in the College was down stairs. A tailor named
Giovanni an Italian lived there too: made clothes for
Mr. Jefferson & his servants. Mrs. Jefferson was there with
Patsy & Polly (Maria). Mrs. Jefferson was small: She
drawed from Old Madam Byrd [5] several hundred people
& then married a rich man. (Bathurst Skelton). Old master had twelve quarters seated with black people: but
mighty few come by him: he want rich himself—only his
larnin. Patsy Jefferson was tall like her father; Polly low
like her mother & longways the handsomest: pretty lady

[4] The Rev. Wm. Douglas in a school at Shadwell near Monticello, instructed
young Jefferson in the rudiments of Greek, Latin & French.
[5] Robert Beverley the historian married Ursula Byrd of Westover, from whom
the Monticello Ursula may have derived her name.

jist like her mother: pity she died—poor thing! She married John W. Eppes—a handsome man, but had a hare-lip.

Jupiter & John drove Mr. Jeffersons coach & four: one of em rode postilion: they rode postilion in them days. Travelling in the phaeton Mr. Jefferson used oftentimes to take the reins himself & drive. Whenever he wanted to travel fast he'd drive: would drive powerful hard himself. Jupiter & John wore caps & gilded bands. The names of the horses was Senegore, Gustavus, Otter, Remus, Romulus & Caractacus Mr. Jefferson's riding-horse.

CHAPTER 3

After one year the Government was moved from Williamsburg to Richmond. Mr. Jefferson moved there with his servants, among em Isaac. It was cold weather when they moved up. Mr. Jefferson lived in a wooden house near where the Palace (Governor's house) stands now. Richmond was a small place then: not more than two brick houses in the town: all wooden houses what there was. At that time from where the Powhatan house now stands clear down to the Old Market was pretty much in pines. It was a wooden house shedded round like a barn on the hill, where the Assemblymen used to meet, near where the Capitol stands now. Old Mr. Wiley had a saddler-shop in the same house. Isaac knew Billy Wiley mighty well—a saddler by trade: he was doorkeeper at the Assembly. His wife was a baker & baked bread & ginger-cakes. Isaac would go into the bake oven & make fire for; she had a great big bake oven. Isaac used to go way into the oven: when he came out Billy Wiley would chuck wood in. She sometimes gave Isaac a loaf of bread or a cake. One time she went up to Monticello to see Mr. Jefferson. She saw Isaac there & gave him a ninepence & said, "This is the boy that made fires for me." Mr. Jefferson's family-servants then at the palace were Bob. Hemings, Martin, Jim,—house-servants, Jupiter & John drivers, Mary Hemings & young Betty Hemings seamstress & house-woman, Sukey, Jupiter's wife the cook.

CHAPTER 4

The day before the British (under Arnold) came to Richmond Mr. Jefferson sent off his family in the carriage. Bob Hemings & Jim drove. When the British was expected (Jan. 6, 1781) Old master kept the spy-glass & git up by the skylight window to the top of the palace looking towards Williamsburg. Some Other gentlemen went up with him, one of them old Mr. Marsdell: he owned where the basin is now & the basin-spring. Isaac used to fetch water from there up to the palace. The British reached Manchester about 1 o'clock.[6] Isaac larnt to beat drum about this time. Bob Anderson a white man was a blacksmith. Mat. Anderson was a black man & worked with Bob. Bob was a fifer Mat was a drummer. Mat bout that time was sort a-makin love to Mary Hemings. The soldiers at Richmond, in the camp at Bacon Quarter Branch would come every two or three days to salute the Governor at the Palace, marching about there drumming & fifing. Bob Anderson would go into the house to drink; Mat went into the kitchen to see Mary Hemings. He would take his drum with him into the kitchen & set it down there. Isaac would beat on it & Mat larnt him how to beat.

CHAPTER 5

As soon as the British formed a line three cannon was wheeled round all at once & fired three rounds. Till they fired the Richmond people thought they was a company

---

[6] They didn't come by way of Manchester.

come from Petersburg to join them: some of em even
hurraed when they see them coming: but that moment
they fired every body knew it was the British. One of the
cannon-balls knocked off the top of a butcher's house:
he was named Daly not far from the Governor's house.
The butcher's wife screamed out & hollerd & her children too & all. In ten minutes not a white man was to be
seen in Richmond: they ran as hard as they could stave
to the camp at Bacon Quarter Branch. There was a monstrous hollering & screaming of women & children. Isaac
was out in the yard: his mother ran out & cotch him up
by the hand & carried him into the kitchen hollering.
Mary Hemings, she jerked up her daughter the same way.
Isaac run out again in a minute & his mother too: she
was so skeered, she did'nt know whether to stay indoors
or out. The British was dressed in red. Isaac saw them
marching. The horsemen (Simcoe's cavalry) was with
them: they come arter the artillerymen. They formed in
line & marched up to the Palace with drums beating: it
was an awful sight: seemed like the day of judgment was
come. When they fired the cannon Old master called out
to John to fetch his horse Caractacus from the stable &
rode off.

CHAPTER 6

Isaac never see his old master arter dat for six months.
When the British come in, an officer rode up & asked
"Whar is the Governor?" Isaac's father (George) told
him:—"He's gone to the mountains." The officer said,
"Whar is the keys of the house?" Isaac's father gave him
the keys: Mr. Jefferson had left them with him. The officer said: "Whar is the silver?" Isaac's father told him,
"It was all sent up to the mountains." The old man had
put all the silver about the house in a bedtick & hid it
under a bed in the kitchen & saved it too & got his free-

dom by it. But he continued to sarve Mr. Jefferson & had forty pounds from old master & his wife. Isaac's mother had seven dollars a month for lifetime for washing, ironing, & making pastry. The British sarcht the house but didn't disturb none of the furniture: but they plundered the wine-cellar, rolled the pipes out & stove em in, knockin the heads out. The bottles they broke the necks off with their swords, drank some, threw the balance away. The wine-cellar was full: old master had plenty of wine & rum—the best: used to have Antigua rum—twelve years old. The British next went to the corn-crib & took all the corn out, strewed it in a line along the street towards where the Washington tavern[7] is now (1847) & brought their horses & fed them on it: took the bridles off. The British said they did'nt want anybody but the Governor: did'nt want to hurt him; only wanted to put a pair of silver handcuffs on him: had brought them along with them on purpose. While they was plunderin they took all of the meat out of the meat-house; cut it up, laid it out in parcels: every man took his ration & put it in his knapsack. When Isaac's mother found they was gwine to car him away she thought they was gwine to leave her: She was cryin & hollerin when one of the officers came on a horse & ordered us all to Hylton's. Then they marched off to Westham. Isaac heard the powder-magazine when it blew up—like an earthquake. Next morning between eight & nine they marched to Tuckahoe, fifteen miles: took a good many colored people from Old Tom. Mann Randolph. He was called "Tuckahoe Tom." Isaac has often been to Tuckahoe—a low-built house, but monstrous large. From Tuckahoe the British went to Daniel Hylton's. They carried off thirty people from Tuckahoe & some from Hylton's. When they come back to Richmond they took all old master's from his house: all of em had to

---

[7] At East end of Grace St.—now (1871) the Central Hotel.

walk except Daniel & Molly (children of Mary the pastry-
cook) & Isaac. He was then big enough to beat the drum:
but could'nt raise it off the ground: would hold it tilted
over to one side & beat on it that way.

CHAPTER 7

There was about a dozen wagons along: they (the
British) pressed the common wagons: four horses to a
wagon: some black drivers, some white: every wagon
guarded by ten men marching alongside.

One of the officers give Isaac name Sambo: all the
time feedin him: put a cocked hat on his head & a red
coat on him & all laughed. Coat a monstrous great big
thing: when Isaac was in it could'nt see nothing of it but
the sleeves dangling down. He remembers crossing the
river somewhere in a periauger (piragua). And so the
British carred them all down to Little York (Yorktown).
They marched straight through town & camped jist below back of the battle-field. Mr. Jefferson's people there
was Jupiter, Sukey the cook, Usley (Isaac's mother)
George (Isaac's father) Mary the seamstress & children
Molly, Daniel, Joe, Wormley, & Isaac. The British treated
them mighty well, give em plenty of fresh meat & wheat
bread. It was very sickly at York: great many colored
people died there, but none of Mr. Jefferson's folks.
Wallis (Cornwallis) had a cave dug & was hid in there.
There was tremendous firing & smoke: seemed like heaven
& earth was come together: every time the great guns
fire Isaac jump up off the ground. Heard the wounded
men hollerin: When the smoke blow off you see the dead
men laying on the ground. General Washington brought
all Mr. Jefferson's folks & about twenty of Tuckahoe Tom's
(Tom Mann Randolph's) back to Richmond with him &
sent word to Mr. Jefferson to send down to Richmond
for his servants. Old master sent down two wagons right

away & all of em that was carred away went up back to Monticello. At that time old master & his family was at Poplar Forest his place in Bedford. He stayed there after his arm was broke, when Caractacus threw him. Old master was mightly pleased to see his people come back safe & sound (Although "All men by nature are free & equal.") & to hear of the plate.

CHAPTER 8

Mr. Jefferson was a tall strait-bodied man as ever you see, right square-shouldered: nary man in this town walked so straight as my old master: neat a built man as ever was seen in Vaginny, I reckon or any place—a straight-up man:[8] long face, high nose.

Jefferson Randolph (Mr. Jefferson's grandson) nothing like him, except in height—tall, like him: not built like him: old master was a Straight-up man. Jefferson Randolph pretty much like his mother. Old master wore Vaginny cloth & a Red Waistcoat, (all the gentlemen wore red waistcoats in dem days) & small clothes: arter dat he used to wear red breeches too.[9] Governor Page used to come up there to Monticello, wife & daughter wid him: drove four-in-hand: servants John, Molly & a postilion. Patrick Henry visited old master: coach & two: his face for all the world like the images of Bonaparte: would stay a week or more. Mann Page used to beat Monticello—a plain mild-looking man: his wife & daughter along with him. Dr. Thomas Walker lived about ten miles from Monticello—a thin-faced man. John

---

[8] Capt. Bacon describes him as "Six feet two & a half inches high, well proportioned & straight as a gun-barrel. He was like a fine horse: he had no surplus flesh."

[9] Capt. Bacon says: "He was always very neat in his dress: wore short breeches & bright shoe-buckles. When he rode on horseback he had a pair of overalls that he always put on."

Walker[10] (of Belvoir), his brother, owned a great many black people.

CHAPTER 9

Old master was never seen to come out before breakfast —about 8 o'clock. If it was warm weather he would'nt ride out till evening: studied upstairs till bell ring for dinner. When writing he had a copyin machine: while he was a-writin he would'nt suffer nobody to come in his room: had a dumb-waiter: When he wanted anything he had nothin to do but turn a crank & the dumb-waiter would bring him water or fruit on a plate or anything he wanted. Old master had abundance of books: sometimes would have twenty of 'em down on the floor at once: read fust one, then tother. Isaac has often wondered how old master came to have such a mighty head: read so many of them books: & when they go to him to ax him anything, he go right straight to the book & tell you all about it. He talked French & Italian. Madzay[11] talked with him: his place was called Colle. General Redhazel (Riedesel) stayed there. He (Mazzei) lived at Monticello with old master some time: Didiot a Frenchman married his daughter Peggy: a heavy chunky looking woman—mighty handsome: She had a daughter Frances & a son Francis: called the daughter Franky. Mazzei brought to Monticello Antonine, Jovanini, Francis, Modena & Belligrini, all gardiners. My old master's garden was monstrous large: two rows of palings, all round ten feet high.

---

[10] John Walker member of Congress during the Revolution.

[11] Philip Mazzei—an Italian—author of "Recherches Sur Les Etats-Unis," 3 Vols. published at Paris, in 1788.

CHAPTER 10

Mr. Jefferson had a clock in his kitchen at Monticello; never went into the kitchen except to wind up the clock. He never would have less than eight covers at dinner—if nobody at table but himself; had from eight to thirty two covers for dinner; plenty of wine, best old Antigua rum & cider: very fond of wine & water, Isaac never heard of his being disguised in drink. He kept three fiddles: played in the arternoons & sometimes arter supper. This was in his early time: When he begin to git so old he did'nt play: kept a spinnet made mostly in shape of a harpsichord: his daughter played on it. Mr. Fauble a Frenchman that lived at Mr. Walker's—a music-man used to come to Monticello & tune it. There was a forte piano & a guitar there: never seed anybody play on them but the French people. Isaac never could git acquainted with them: could hardly larn their names. Mr. Jefferson always singing when ridin or walkin; hardly see him anywhar out doors but what he was a-singin.[12] Had a fine clear voice, sung minnits (minuets) & sich: fiddled in the parlor. Old master very kind to servants.

CHAPTER 11

The fust year Mr. Jefferson was elected President, he took Isaac on to Philadelphia: he was then about fifteen years old: travelled on horseback in company with a Frenchman named Joseph Rattiff & Jim Hemings a body-servant. Fust day's journey they went from Monticello to old Nat. Gordon's on the Fredericksburg road next day to Fredericksburg, then to Georgetown, crossed the Potomac there, & so to Philadelphia: eight days a-goin. Had two

[12] Capt. Bacon says: "When he was not talking he was nearly always humming some tune; or singing in a low tone to himself."

ponies & Mr. Jefferson's tother riding-horse Odin. Mr. Jefferson went in the phaeton: Bob. Hemings drove: changed horses on the road. When they got to Philadelphia Isaac stayed three days at Mr. Jefferson's house: then he was bound prentice to one Bringhouse a tinner: he lived in the direction of the Water-works. Isaac remembers seeing the image of a woman thar holding a goose in her hand—the water spouting out of the goose's mouth. This was at the head of Market Street. Bringhouse was a short mighty small neat-made man: treated Isaac very well: went thar to larn the tinner's trade: fust week larnt to cut out & sodder. make little pepper-boxes & graters & sich, out of scraps of tin, so as not to wast any till he had larnt. Then to making cups. Every Sunday Isaac would go to the President's House—large brick house, many windows: same house Ginral Washington lived in before when he was President. "Old master used to talk to me mighty free & ax me, how you come on Isaac, larnin de tin-business?" As soon as he could make cups pretty well he carred three or four to show him. Isaac made four dozen pint-cups a day & larnt to tin copper & sheets (sheet-iron)—make 'em tin. He lived four years with Old Bringhouse. One time Mr. Jefferson sent to Bringhouse to tin his copper-kittles & pans for kitchen use: Bringhouse sent Isaac & another prentice thar—a white boy named Charles: cant think of his other name. Isaac was the only black boy in Bringhouse's Shop. When Isaac carred the cups to his old master to show him he was mightily pleased: said, "Isaac you are larnin mighty fast: I bleeve I must send you back to Vaginny to car on the tin-business. You is growin too big: no use for you to stay here no longer." Arter dat Mr. Jefferson sent Isaac back to Monticello to car on the tin-business thar. Old master bought a sight of tin for the purpose. Mr. Jefferson had none of his family with him in Philadelphia. Polly his daughter stayed with her Aunt Patsy Carr: she lived

seven or eight miles from old master's great house. Sam.
Carr was Mr. Jefferson's sister's child. There were three
brothers of the Carrs—Sam, Peter & Dabney. Patsy Jefferson while her father was President in Philadelphia stayed
with Mrs. Eppes at Wintopoke: Mrs. Eppes was a sister
of Mrs. Jefferson:—Mightily like her sister. Frank Eppes
was a big heavy man.

Old master's servants at Philadelphia was Bob. & Jim
Hemings, Joseph Ratiff a Frenchman—the hostler. Mr.
Jefferson used to ride out on horseback in Philadelphia.
Isaac went back to Monticello. When the tin came they
fixed up a shop. Jim Bringhouse came on to Monticello
all the way with old master to fix up the shop & start Isaac
to work: Jim. Bringhouse stayed thar more than a month.

CHAPTER 12

Isaac knew old Colonel (Archibald) Cary mighty well:
as dry a looking man as ever you see in your life. He has
given Isaac more whippings than he has fingers & toes.
Mr. Jefferson used to set Isaac to open gates for Col.
Cary: there was three gates to open, the furst bout a mile
from the house: tother one three quarters; then the yard-
gate, at the stable three hundred yards from the house:
Isaac had to open the gates. Col. Cary would write to old
master what day he was coming. Whenever Isaac missed
opening them gates in time, the Colonel soon as he git to
the house, look about for him & whip him with his horse-
whip. Old master used to keep dinner for Col. Cary. He
was a tall thin-visaged man jist like Mr. Jefferson: he
drove four-in-hand. The Colonel as soon as he git out of
his carriage, walk right straight into the kitchen & ax de
cooks what they hab for dinner? If they did'nt have what
he wanted—bleeged to wait dinner till it was cooked. Col.
Cary made freer at Monticello than he did at home: whip
anybody: would stay several weeks: give servants money,

sometimes five or six dollars among 'em. Tuckahoe Tom
Randolph married Col. Cary's daughter Nancy. The Colo-
nel lived at Ampthill on the James river where Col. Bob.
Temple lived arterwards. Edgehill was the seat of Tom.
Mann Randolph father of Jefferson Randolph: it was three
miles from Monticello.

CHAPTER 13

Isaac carried on the tin-business two years:—it failed. He
then carred on the nail-business at Monticello seven years:
made money at that. Mr. Jefferson had the first (nail) cutting machine 'twas said, that ever was in Vaginny,—sent
over from England: made wrought nails & cut-nails, to
single & lathe: sold them out of the shop: got iron rods
from Philadelphia by water: boated them up from Richmond to Milton a small town on the Rivanna: wagoned
from thar.

CHAPTER 14

Thomas Mann Randolph had ten children.[13] Isaac lived
with him fust & last twenty six or seven years: treated
him mighty well: one of the finest masters in Virginia: his
a wife mighty peaceable woman: never holler for servant:
make no fuss nor racket: pity she ever died! Tom Mann
Randolph's eldest daughter Ann: a son named Jefferson,
another James & another Benjamin: Jefferson Randolph
married Mr. Nicholas'[14] daughter (Anne). Billy Giles[15]
courted Miss Polly old master's daughter. Isaac one morning saw him talking to her in the garden, right back of the

---

[13] Thomas Mann Randolph's sons were Thomas Jefferson, James Madison
Benjamin Franklin, Merriwether Lewis & George Wythe (Secy. of War. of
C. S.) daughters Anne, Ellen, Virginia, Cornelia & Septimia.

[14] Wilson Cary Nicholas, sometime Governor of Virginia.

[15] Wm C Giles. M. C. a celebrated debater. Sometime Governor of Virginia.
He acquired the sobriquet of "Farmer Giles."

nail-factory shop: she was lookin on de ground: all at once she wheeled round & come off. That was the time she turned him off. Isaac never so sorry for a man in all his life: sorry because every body thought she was going to marry him. Mr. Giles give several dollars to the servants & when he went away dat time he never come back no more. His servant Arthur was a big man. Isaac wanted Mr. Giles to marry Miss Polly. Arthur always said that he was a mighty fine man: he was very rich: used to come to Monticello in a monstrous fine gig: mighty few gigs in dem days with plated mountins & harness.

CHAPTER 15

Elk Hill: old master had a small brick house there where he used to stay, about a mile from Elk Island on the North Side of the James river. The river forks there: one half runs one side of the island, tother the other side. When Mr. Jefferson was Governor he used to stay thar a month or sich a matter & when he was at the mountain he would come & stay a month or so & then go back again. Blenheim was a low large wooden house two storeys high, eight miles from Monticello. Old. Col. Carter lived thar: had a light red head like Mr. Jefferson: Isaac know'd him & every son he had:—did'nt know his daughters.

Mr. Jefferson used to hunt squirrels & partridges; kept five or six guns; oftentimes carred Isaac wid him: old master would'nt shoot partridges settin: said "he would'nt take advantage of em"—would give 'em a chance for thar life: would'nt shoot a hare settin, nuther; skeer him up fust. "My old master was as neat a hand as ever you see to make keys & locks & small chains, iron & brass:" he kept all kind of blacksmith and carpenter tools in a great case with shelves to it in his library—an upstairs room. Isaac went up thar constant: been up thar a thousand times; used to car coal up thar: old master had a couple of small bellowses up thar. The likeness of Mr. Jefferson (in Linn's Life of him) according to Isaac, is not much like him. "Old master never dat handsome in dis world: dat likeness right between old master & Ginral Washington: old master was squar-shouldered." For amusement he would work sometimes in the garden for half an hour at a time in right good earnest in the cool of the evening: never know'd him to go out anywhar before breakfast.

CHAPTER 16

The school at Monticello was in the out-chamber fifty yards off from the great house, on the same level. But the scholars went into the house to old master to git lessons— in the South eend of the house called the South Octagon. Mrs. Skipper (Skipwith) had two daughters thar: Mrs. Eppes, one.

Mr. Jefferson's sister Polly married old Ned Bolling[16] of Chesterfield about ten miles from Petersburg. Isaac has been thar since his death: saw the old man's grave. Mr. John Bradley owns the place now. Isaac slept in the out-chamber where the scholars was: slept on the floor in a blanket: in the winter season git up in the morning & make fire for them. From Monticello you can see mountains all round as far as the eye can reach: sometimes see it rainin down this course & the sun shining over the tops of the clouds. Willis' mountain sometimes looked in the cloud like a great house with two chimnies to it: fifty miles from Monticello.

CHAPTER 17

Thar was a sight of pictures at Monticello: pictures of Ginral Washington & the Marcus Lafayette. Isaac saw

[16] John Bolling of Cobbs in Chesterfield married a sister of Thomas Jefferson.

him fust in the old war in the mountain with old master; saw him agin the last time he was in Vaginny. He gave Isaac a guinea: Isaac saw him in the Capitol at Richmond & talked with him & made him sensible when he fust saw him in the old war. Thar was a large marble at Monticello with twelve angels cut on it that came from Heaven: all cut in marble.

About the time when "my old master" begun to wear spectacles, he was took with a swellin in his legs: used to bathe 'em & bandage 'em: said it was setting too much: when he'd git up & walk it would'nt hurt him. Isaac & John Hemings nursed him two months: had to car him about on a han-barrow. John Hemings[17] went to the carpenter's trade same year Isaac went to the blacksmiths. Miss Lucy old master's daughter died quite a small child; died down the country at Mrs. Eppes' or Mrs. Bollings one of her young aunts. Old master was embassador to France at that time. He brought a great many clothes from France with him: a coat of blue cloth trimmed with gold lace; cloak trimmed so too: dar say it weighed fifty pounds: large buttons on the coat as big as half a dollar; cloth set in the button: edge shine like gold: in summer he war silk coat, pearl buttons.

Col. Jack Harvie[18] owned Belmont jinin Monticello. Four as big men as any in Petersburg could git in his waistcoat: he owned Belvidere near Richmond: the Colonel died thar: monstrous big man. The washerwoman once buttoned his waistcoat on Isaac & three others. Mrs. Harvie was a little woman.

---

[17] Capt. Bacon in his reminiscenses of Mr. Jefferson at Monticello says, "John Hemings was a carpenter. He was a first-rate workman, a very extra workman: he could make anything that was wanting in woodwork. He learned his trade with Dinsmore. John Hemings made most of the woodwork of Mr. Jefferson's fine carriage."

[18] He had command of the troops of Convention, for a time.

CHAPTER 18

Mr. Jefferson never had nothing to do with horse-racing or cock-fighting: bought two race horses once, but not in their racing day: bought em arter done runnin. One was Brimmer,[19] a pretty horse with two white feet: when he bought him he was in Philadelphia: kept him thar. One day Joseph Rattiff the Frenchman was ridin him in the Streets of Philadelphia: Brimmer got skeered: run agin shaft of a dray & got killed. Tother horse was Tarkill: (Tarquin?) in his race-day they called him the Roane colt: only race-horse of a roane Isaac ever see: old master used him for a ridin-horse. Davy Watson & Billy were German soldiers: both workmen, both smoked pipes & both drinkers: drank whiskey: git drunk & sing: take a week at a time drinkin & singin. Col. Goode of Chesterfield was a great racer: used to visit Mr. Jefferson; had a trainer named Pompey.

Old master had a great many rabbits: made chains for the old buck-rabbits to keep them from killin the young ones: had a rabbit-house (a warren)—a long rock house: some of em white, some blue: they used to burrow under ground. Isaac expects thar is plenty of em bout dar yit: used to eat em at Monticello. Mr. Jefferson never danced nor played cards. He had dogs named Ceres, Bull, Armandy, & Claremont: most of em French dogs: he brought em over with him from France. Bull & Ceres were bull-dogs: he brought over Buzzy with him too: she pupped at Sea: Armandy & Claremont, Stump-tails—both black.

---

[19] According to Capt. Bacon. "Brimmer was a son of imported Knowlsby. He was a bay, but a shade darker than any of the others. He was a horse of fair size, full, but not quite as tall as Eagle. He was a good riding-horse & excellent for the harness. Mr. Jefferson broke all his horses to both ride & work. I bought Brimmer of General John H. Cocke of Fluvanna County."

CHAPTER 19

John Brock the overseer that lived next to the great-house had gray hounds to hunt deer. Mr. Jefferson had a large park at Monticello: built in a sort of a flat on the side of the mountain. When the hunters ran the deer down thar, they'd jump into the park & could'nt git out. When old master heard hunters in the park he used to go down thar wid his gun & order em out. The park was two or three miles round & fenced in with a high fence, twelve rails double-staked & ridered: kept up four or five years arter old master was gone: Isaac & his father (George) fed the deer at sun-up & sun-down: called em up & fed em wid corn: had holes all along the fence at the feedin-place: gave em salt, got right gentle: come up & eat out of your hand.

No wild-cats at Monticello: some lower down at Buck Island: bears sometimes came on the plantation at Monticello: wolves so plenty that they had to build pens around black peoples' quarters & pen sheep in em to keep the wolves from catching them. But they killed five or six of a night in the winter season: come & steal in the pens in the night. When the snow was on the groun you could see the wolves in gangs runnin & howlin, same as a drove of hogs: made the deer run up to the feedin-place many a night. The feedin place was right by the house whar Isaac stayed. They raised many sheep & goats at Monticello.

The woods & mountains was often on fire: Isaac has gone out to help to put out the fire: everybody would turn out from Charlottesville & everywhere: git in the woods & sometimes work all night fightin the fire.

CHAPTER 20

Col. Cary of Chesterfield schooled old master: he went to school to old Mr. Wayles. Old master had six sisters: Polly married a Bolling; Patsy married old Dabney Carr in the low-grounds: one married Wm. Skipwith: Nancy married old Hastings Marks. Old master's brother, Mass Randall, (Randolph) was a mighty simple man: used to come out among black people, play the fiddle & dance half the night: had'nt much more sense than Isaac. Jack Eppes (John W. Eppes M. C.) that married Miss Polly (Jefferson) lived at Mount Black (Mt. Blanc?) on James river & then at Edge Hill, then in Cumberland at Millbrooks. Isaac left Monticello four years before Mr. Jefferson died. Tom Mann Randolph that married Mr. Jefferson's daughter, wanted Isaac to build a threshing machine at Varina. Old Henrico Court House was thar: pulled down now. Coxendale Island (Dutch Gap) jinin Varina was an Indian Situation: when fresh come, it washed up more Indian bones than ever you see. When Isaac was a boy there want more than ten houses at Jamestown. Charlottesville then not as big as Pocahontas (a village on the Appomattox, opposite Petersburg) is now. Mr. DeWitt kept tavern thar.

Isaac knowed Ginral Redhazel (Riedesel commander of the German troops of Convention.): he stayed at Colle, Mr. Mazzei's place, two miles & a quarter from Monticello —a long wood house built by Mazzei's servants. The servants' house built of little saplins of oak & hickory instead of lathes: then plastered up: it seemed as if de folks in dem days had'nt sense enough to make lathes. The Italian people raised plenty of vegetables: cooked the most victuals of any people Isaac ever see.

Mr. Jefferson bowed to everybody he meet: talked wid his arms folded. Gave the boys in the nail-factory a pound of meat a week, a dozen herrings, a quart of molasses &

peck of meal. Give them that wukked the best a suit of red or blue: encouraged them mightily. Isaac calls him a mighty good master. There would be a great many carriages at Monticello at a time, in particular when people was passing to the Springs.

Isaac is now (1847) at Petersburg, Va. seventy large odd years old: bears his years well: is a blacksmith by trade & has his shop not far from Pockahontas bridge. He is quite pleased at the idea of having his life written & protests that every word of it is true, that is of course according to the best of his knowledge & belief. Isaac is rather tall of strong frame, stoops a little, in color ebony:— sensible, intelligent pleasant: wears large circular ironbound spectacles & a leather apron. A capital daguerrotype of him was taken by a Mr. Shew. Isaac was so much pleased with it that he had one taken of his wife, a large fat round-faced good-humoured looking black woman. My attention was first drawn to Isaac by Mr. Dandridge Spotswood who had often heard him talk about Mr. Jefferson & Monticello.

C. C.

P.S. Isaac died a few years after these his recollections were taken down. He bore a good character.

2

FROM

Narrative of the Life of Frederick Douglass, An American Slave written by himself

(1817?–1895)

This selection is of interest for several reasons: it gives a vivid description of the cruelties of slavery on a Maryland plantation from the perspective of a young boy; it provides an account of the life of a slave in the city with comparisons to that of a rural slave; and it offers another example of the stirring determination with which some slaves pursued the golden dream of education. Finally, it gives a penetrating insight into the effects of slaveholding upon the owner, as we witness the rapid degradation of a decent family when confronted with the arbitrary power of human bondage.

Frederick Douglass never knew the exact year of his birth, but overheard his first owner say it was 1817 or 1818. When he was sent to Baltimore as a young boy it was to the house of people who had never before been slaveholders. There, in an unusual act of kindness, his mistress taught him to read.

He escaped to New York City in 1838 and married a free Negro woman whom he had met in Baltimore. He agi-

*tated for abolition before the war, recruited Negro sol-
diers during it, and fought for the rights of the newly
freed black population after it was over.*

*Later he was appointed Secretary of the Santo Do-
mingo Commission, Marshal and Recorder of Deeds in
the District of Columbia and United States Minister to
Haiti.*

I WAS born in Tuckahow, near Hillsborough, and about
twelve miles from Easton, in Talbot county, Maryland. I
have no accurate knowledge of my age, never having seen
any authentic record containing it. By far the larger part
of the slaves know as little of their ages as horses know of
theirs, and it is the wish of most masters within my knowledge to keep their slaves thus ignorant. I do not remember to have ever met a slave who tells of his birthday.
They seldom come nearer to it than planting-time. A want
of information concerning my own was a source of unhap-
piness to me even during childhood. The white children
could tell their ages. I could not tell why I ought to be deprived of the same privilege. I was not allowed to make
any inquiries of my master concerning it. He deemed all
such inquiries on the part of a slave improper and im-
pertinent, and evidence of a restless spirit. The nearest
estimate I can give makes me now between twenty-seven
and twenty-eight years of age. I come to this, from hearing my master say, some time during 1835, I was about
seventeen years old.

My mother was named Harriet Bailey. She was the
daughter of Isaac and Betsey Bailey, both colored, and
quite dark. My mother was of a darker complexion than
either my grandmother or grandfather.

My father was a white man. He was admitted to be
such by all I ever heard speak of my parentage. The opinion was also whispered that my master was my father;
but of the correctness of this opinion, I know nothing; the

means of knowing was withheld from me. My mother and I were separated when I was but an infant—before I knew her as my mother. It is a common custom, in the part of Maryland from which I ran away, to part children from their mothers at a very early age. Frequently, before the child has reached its twelfth month, its mother is taken from it, and hired on some farm a considerable distance off, and the child is placed under the care of an old woman, too old for field labor. For what this separation is done, I do not know, unless it be to hinder the development of the child's affection toward its mother, and to blunt and destroy the natural affection of the mother for the child. This is the inevitable result.

I never saw my mother, to know her as such, more than four or five times in my life; and each of these times was very short in duration, and at night. She was hired by Mr. Stewart, who lived about twelve miles from my home. She made her journeys to see me in the night, travelling the whole distance on foot, after the performance of her day's work. She was a field hand, and a whipping is the penalty of not being in the field at sunrise, unless a slave has special permission from his or her master to the contrary—a permission which they seldom get, and one that gives to him that gives it the proud name of being a kind master. I do not recollect of ever seeing my mother by the light of day. She was with me in the night. She would lie down with me, and get me to sleep, but long before I waked she was gone. Very little communication ever took place between us. Death soon ended what little we could have while she lived, and with it her hardships and suffering. She died when I was about seven years old, on one of my master's farms, near Lee's Mill. I was not allowed to be present during her illness, at her death, or burial. She was gone long before I knew anything about it. Never having enjoyed, to any considerable extent, her soothing presence, her tender and watchful care, I received the tidings of her death with much the same emotions I should have probably felt at the death of a stranger.

Called thus suddenly away, she left me without the slightest intimation of who my father was. The whisper that my master was my father, may or may not be true; and, true or false, it is of but little consequence to my purpose whilst the fact remains, in all its glaring odiousness, that slaveholders have ordained, and by law established, that the children of slave women shall in all cases follow the condition of their mothers; and this is done too obviously to administer to their own lusts, and make a gratification of their wicked desires profitable as well as pleasurable, for by this cunning arrangement, the slaveholder, in cases not a few, sustains to his slaves the double relation of master and father.

I know of such cases; and it is worthy of remark that such slaves invariably suffer greater hardships, and have more to contend with, than others. They are, in the first place, a constant offense to their mistress. She is ever disposed to find fault with them; they can seldom do any thing to please her; she is never better pleased than when she sees them under the lash, especially when she suspects her husband of showing to his mulatto children favors which he withholds from his black slaves. The master is frequently compelled to sell this class of his slaves, out of deference to the feelings of his white wife; and cruel as the deed may strike any one to be, for a man to sell his own children to human flesh-mongers, it is often the dictate of humanity for him to do so; for, unless he does this, he must not only whip them himself, but must stand by and see one white son tie up his brother, of but few shades darker complexion than himself, and ply the gory lash to his naked back; and if he lisp one word of disapproval, it is set down to his parental partiality, and only makes a bad matter worse, both for himself and the slave whom he would protect and defend.

Every year brings with it multitudes of this class of slaves. It was doubtless in consequence of a knowledge of this fact, that one great statesman of the south predicted the downfall of slavery by the inevitable laws of population. Whether this prophecy is ever fulfilled or not, it is nevertheless plain that a very different-looking class of people are springing up at the south, and are now held in slavery, from those originally brought to this country from Africa; and if their increase will do no other good, it will do away the force of the argument, that God cursed Ham, and therefore American slavery is right. If the lineal descendants of Ham are alone to be scripturally enslaved, it is certain that slavery at the south must soon become unscriptural; for thousands are ushered into the world, annually, who, like myself, owe their existence to white fathers, and those fathers most frequently their own masters.

I have had two masters. My first master's name was Anthony. I do not remember his first name. He was generally called Captain Anthony—a title which, I presume, he acquired by sailing a craft on the Chesapeake Bay. He was not considered a rich slaveholder. He owned two or three farms, and about thirty slaves. His farms and slaves were under the care of an overseer. The overseer's name was Plummer. Mr. Plummer was a miserable drunkard, a profane swearer, and a savage monster. He always went armed with a cowskin and a heavy cudgel. I have known him to cut and slash the women's heads so horribly, that even master would be enraged at his cruelty, and would threaten to whip him if he did not mind himself. Master, however, was not a humane slaveholder. It required extraordinary barbarity on the part of an overseer to affect him. He was a cruel man, hardened by a long life of slaveholding. He would at times seem to take great pleasure in whipping a slave. I have often been awakened at the dawn of day by the most heart-rending shrieks of an own aunt of mine, whom he used to tie up to a joist, and whip upon her naked back til she was literally covered with blood. No words, no tears, no prayers, from his gory victim, seemed to move his iron heart from its bloody purpose. The louder she screamed, the harder he whipped; and where the blood ran fastest, there he whipped longest. He would whip her to make her scream, and whip her to make her hush; and not until overcome by fatigue, would he cease to swing the blood-clotted cowskin. I remember the first time I ever witnessed this horrible exhibition. I was quite a child, but I will remember it. I never shall forget it whilst I remember anything. It was the first of a long series of such outrages, of which I was doomed to be a witness and a participant. It struck me with awful force. It was the blood-stained gate, the entrance to the hell of slavery, through which I was about to pass. It was a most terrible spectacle. I wish I could commit to paper the feelings with which I beheld it.

This occurrence took place very soon after I went to live with my old master, and under the following circumstances. Aunt Hester went out one night—where or for what I do not know,—and happened to be absent when my master desired her presence. He had ordered her not to go out evenings, and warned her that she must never let him catch her in company with a young man, who was paying attention to her belonging to Colonel Lloyd. The young man's name was Ned Roberts, generally called Lloyd's Ned. Why master was so careful of her, may be safely left to conjecture. She was a woman of noble form, and of graceful proportions, having very few equals, and fewer superiors, in personal appearance, among the colored or white women of our neighborhood.

Aunt Hester had not only disobeyed his orders in going out, but had been found in company with Lloyd's Ned; which circumstance, I found, from what he said while whipping her, was the chief offence. Had he been a man of pure morals himself, he might have been thought interested in protecting the innocence of my aunt; but those who knew him will not suspect him of any such virtue. Before he commenced whipping Aunt Hester, he took her into the kitchen, and stripped her from neck to waist, leaving her neck, shoulders, and back entirely naked. He then told her to cross her hands, calling her at the same time a d—d b—h. After crossing her hands, he tied them with a strong rope, and led her to a stool under a large hook in the joist, put in for the purpose. He made her get upon the stool, and tied her hands to the hook. She now stood fair for his infernal purpose. Her arms were stretched up at their full length, so that she stood upon the ends of her toes. He then said to her, "Now you d—d b—h, I'll learn you how to disobey my orders!" and after rolling up his sleeves, he commenced to lay on the heavy cowskin, and soon the warm, red blood (amid heart-rending shrieks from her, and horrid oaths from him) came dripping to the floor. I was so terrified and horror stricken at the sight, that I hid myself in a closet, and dared not venture out till long after the bloody transaction was over. I expected it would be my turn next. It was all new to me. I had never seen anything like it before. I had always lived with my grandmother on the outskirts of the plantation, where she was put to raise the children of the younger women. I had therefore been, until now, out of the way of the bloody scenes that often occurred on the plantation.

As to my own treatment while I lived on Colonel Lloyd's plantation, it was very similar to that of the other slave children. I was not old enough to work in the field, and there being little else than field work to do, I had a great deal of leisure time. The most I had to do was to drive up the cows at evening, keep the fowls out of the garden, keep the front yard clean, and run errands for my old master's daughter, Mrs. Lucretia Auld. The most of my leisure time I spent in helping Master Daniel Lloyd in finding his birds, after he had shot them. My connection with Master Daniel was of some advantage to me. He became quite attached to me, and was sort of a protector of me. He would not allow the older boys to impose upon me, and would divide his cakes with me.

I was seldom whipped by my old master, and suffered little from anything else than hunger and cold. I suffered much from hunger, but much more from cold. In hottest summer and coldest winter, I was kept almost naked—no shoes, no stockings, no jacket, no trousers, nothing on but a coarse tow linen shirt, reaching only to my knees. I had no bed. I must have perished with cold, but that, the coldest nights, I used to steal a bag which was used for carrying corn to the mill. I would crawl into this bag, and there sleep on the cold, damp, clay floor, with my head in and feet out. My feet have been so cracked with the frost, that the pen with which I am writing might be laid in the gashes.

We were not regularly allowanced. Our food was coarse corn meal boiled. This was called *mush*. It was put into a large wooden tray or trough, and set down upon the ground. The children were then called, like so many pigs, and like so many pigs they would come and devour the mush; some with oyster-shells, others with pieces of shingle, some with naked hands, and none with spoons. He that ate fastest got most; he that was strongest secured the best place; and few left the trough satisfied.

I was probably between seven and eight years old when I left Colonel Lloyd's plantation. I left it with joy. I shall never forget the ecstasy with which I received the intelligence that my old master (Anthony) had determined to let me go to Baltimore, to live with Mr. Hugh Auld, brother to my old master's son-in-law, Captain Thomas Auld. I received this information about three days before my departure. They were three of the happiest days I ever enjoyed. I spent the most part of all these three days in the creek, washing off the plantation scurf, and preparing myself for my departure.

The pride of appearance which this would indicate was not my own. I spent the time in washing, not so much because I wished to, but because Mrs. Lucretia had told me I must get all the dead skin off my feet and knees before I could go to Baltimore; for the people in Baltimore were very cleanly, and would laugh at me if I looked dirty. Besides, she was going to give me a pair of trousers, which I should not put on unless I got all the dirt off me. The thought of owning a pair of trousers was great indeed! It was almost a sufficient motive, not only to make me take off what would be called by pig-drovers the mange, but the skin itself. I went at it in good earnest, working for the first time with the hope of reward.

The ties that ordinarily bind children to their homes were all suspended in my case. I found no severe trial in my departure. My home was charmless; it was not home to me; on parting from it, I could not feel that I was leaving any thing which I could have enjoyed by staying. My mother was dead, my grandmother lived far off, so that I seldom saw her. I had two sisters and one brother, that lived in the same house with me; but the early separation of us from our mother had well nigh blotted the fact of our relationship from our memories. I looked for home elsewhere, and was confident of finding none which I should relish less than the one which I was leaving. If, however, I found in my new home hardship, hunger, whipping, and nakedness, I had the consolation that I should not have escaped any one of them by staying. Having already had more than a taste of them in the house of my old master, and having endured them there, I very naturally inferred my ability to endure them elsewhere, and especially in Baltimore; for I had something of the feeling about Baltimore, that is expressed in the proverb, that "being hanged in England is preferable to dying a natural death in Ireland." I had the strongest desire to see Baltimore. Cousin Tom, though not fluent in speech, had inspired me with that desire by his eloquent description of the place. I could never point out any thing at the Great House, no matter how beautiful or powerful, but that he had seen something at Baltimore far exceeding both in beauty and strength, the object which I pointed out to him. Even the Great House itself, with all its pictures, was far inferior to many buildings in Baltimore. So strong was my desire, that I thought a gratification of it would fully compensate for whatever loss of comforts I should sustain by the exchange. I left without regret, and with the highest hopes of future happiness.

We sailed out of Miles River for Baltimore on a Saturday morning. I remember only the day of the week, for at that time I had no knowledge of the days of the month, nor the months of the year. On setting sail, I walked aft, and gave to Colonel Lloyd's plantation what I hoped would be the last look. I then placed myself in the bows of the sloop, and there spent the remainder of the day in looking ahead, interesting myself in what was in the distance rather than in things near by or behind.

In the afternoon of that day, we reached Annapolis, the capital of the State. We stopped but a few moments, so that I had no time to go on shore. It was the first large town that I had ever seen, and though it would look small compared with some of our New England factory villages, I thought it a wonderful place for its size—more imposing even than the Great House Farm!

We arrived at Baltimore early on Sunday morning, landing at Smith's Wharf, not far from Bowley's Wharf. We had on board the sloop a large flock of sheep; and after aiding in driving them to the slaughterhouse of Mr. Curtis on Loudon Slater's Hill, I was conducted by Rich, one of the hands belonging on board of the sloop, to my new home in Alliciana Street, near Mr. Gardner's shipyard, on Fells Point.

Mr. and Mrs. Auld were both at home, and met me at the door with their little son Thomas, to take care of whom I had been given. And here I saw what I had never seen before; it was a white face beaming with the most kindly emotions; it was the face of my new mistress, Sophia Auld. I wish I could describe the rapture that flashed through my soul as I beheld it. It was a new and strange sight to me, brightening up my pathway with the light of happiness. Little Thomas was told, there was his Freddy—and I was told to take care of little Thomas; and thus I entered upon the duties of my new home with the most cheering prospect ahead.

I looked upon my departure from Colonel Lloyd's plantation as one of the most interesting events of my life. It is possible, and even quite probable, that but for the mere circumstance of being removed from that plantation to Baltimore, I should have to-day, instead of being here seated by my own table, in the enjoyment of freedom and the happiness of home, writing this Narrative, been confined in the galling chains of slavery. Going to live at Baltimore laid the foundation, and opened the gateway, to all my subsequent prosperity. I have ever regarded it as the first plain manifestation of that kind providence which has ever since attended me, and marked my life with so many favors. I regarded the selection of myself as being somewhat remarkable. There were a number of slave children that might have been sent from the plantation to Baltimore. There were those younger, those older, and those of the same age. I was chosen from among them all, and was the first, last, and only choice.

I may be deemed superstitious, and even egotistical, in regarding this event as a special interposition of divine Providence in my favor. But I should be false to the earliest sentiments of my soul, if I suppressed the opinion. I prefer to be true to myself, even at the hazard of incurring the ridicule of others, rather than to be false, and incur my own abhorrence. From my earliest recollection, I date the entertainment of a deep conviction that slavery would not always be able to hold me within its foul embrace; and in the darkest hours of my career in slavery, this living word of faith and spirit of hope departed not from me, but remained like ministering angels to cheer me through the gloom. This good spirit was from God, and to him I offer thanksgiving and praise.

My new mistress proved to be all she appeared when I first met her at the door—a woman of the kindest heart and finest feelings. She had never had a slave under her control previously to myself, and prior to her marriage she had been dependent upon her own industry to get a living. She was by trade a weaver; and by constant application to her business, she had been in a good degree preserved from the blighting and dehumanizing effects of slavery. I was utterly astonished at her goodness. I scarcely knew how to behave towards her. She was entirely unlike any other white woman I had ever seen. I could not approach her as I was accustomed to approach other white ladies. My early instruction was all out of place. The crouching servility, usually so acceptable a quality in a slave, did not answer when manifested toward her. Her favor was not gained by it; she seemed to be disturbed by it. She did not deem it impudent or unmannerly for a slave to look her in the face. The meanest slave was put fully at ease in her presence, and none left without feeling better for having seen her. Her face was made of heavenly smiles, and her voice of tranquil music.

But, alas! this kind heart had but a short time to remain such. The fatal poison of irresponsible power was already in her hands, and soon commenced its infernal work. That cheerful eye, under the influence of slavery, soon became red with rage; that voice, made all of sweet accord, changed to one of harsh and horrid discord; and that angelic face gave place to that of a demon.

Very soon after I went to live with Mr. and Mrs. Auld, she very kindly commenced to teach me the A, B, C. After I had learned this, she assisted me in learning to spell words of three or four letters. Just at this point of my progress, Mr. Auld found out what was going on, and at once forbade Mrs. Auld to instruct me further, telling her, among other things, that it was unlawful, as well as unsafe, to teach a slave to read. To use his own words, further, he said, "If you give a nigger an inch, he will take an ell. A nigger should know nothing but to obey his master —to do as he is told to do. Learning would *spoil* the best nigger in the world. Now," he said, "if you teach that nigger (speaking of myself) how to read, there would be no keeping him. It would be forever unfit for him to be a slave. He would at once become unmanageable, and of no value to his master. As to himself, it could do him no good, but a great deal of harm. It would make him discontented and unhappy." These words sank deep into my heart, stirring up sentiments within that lay slumbering, and called into existence an entirely new train of thought. It was a new and special revelation, explaining dark and mysterious things, with which my youthful understanding had struggled, but struggled in vain. I now understood what had been to me a most perplexing difficulty—to wit, the white man's power to enslave the black man. It was a grand achievement, and I prized it highly. From that moment, I understood the pathway from slavery to freedom. It was just what I wanted, and I got it at a time when I the least expected it. Whilst I was saddened by the thought of losing the aid of my kind mistress, I was gladdened by the invaluable instruction which, by the merest accident, I gained from my master. Though conscious of the difficulty of learning without a teacher, I set out with high hope, and a fixed purpose, at whatever cost of trouble, to learn how to read. The very decided manner with which he spoke, and strove to impress his wife with the evil consequences of giving me instruction, served to convince me that he was deeply sensible of the truths he was uttering. It gave me the best assurance that I might rely with the utmost confidence on the results which, he said, would flow from teaching me to read. What he most dreaded, that I most desired. What he most loved, that I most hated. That which to him was a great evil, to be carefully shunned, was to me a great good, to be diligently sought; and the argument which he so warmly urged, against my learning to read, only served to inspire me with a desire and determination to learn. In learning to read, I owe almost as much to the bitter opposition of my master, as to the kindly aid of my mistress. I acknowledge the benefit of both.

I had resided but a short time in Baltimore before I observed a marked difference, in the treatment of slaves, from that which I had witnessed in the country. A city slave is almost a freeman, compared with a slave on the plantation. He is much better fed and clothed, and enjoys privileges altogether unknown to the slave on the plantation. There is a vestige of decency, a sense of shame, that does much to curb and check those outbreaks of atrocious cruelty so commonly enacted upon the plantation. He is a desperate slaveholder, who will shock the humanity of his non-slaveholding neighbors with cries of his lacerated slave. Few are willing to incur the odium attaching to the reputation of being a cruel master; and above all things, they would not be known as not giving a slave enough to eat. Every city slaveholder is anxious to have it known of him, that he feeds his slaves well; and it is due to them to say, that most of them do give their slaves enough to eat. There are, however, some painful exceptions to this rule. Directly opposite to us, on Philpot Street, lived Mr. Thomas Hamilton. He owned two slaves. Their names were Henrietta and Mary. Henrietta was about twenty-two years of age, Mary was about fourteen; and of all the mangled and emaciated creatures I ever looked upon, these two were the most so. His heart must be harder than stone, that could look upon these unmoved. The head, neck, and shoulders of Mary were literally cut to pieces. I have frequently felt her head, and found it nearly covered with festering sores, caused by the lash of her cruel mistress. I do not know that her master ever whipped her, but I have been an eye-witness to the cruelty of Mrs. Hamilton. I used to be in Mr. Hamilton's house nearly every day. Mrs. Hamilton used to sit in a large chair in the middle of the room, with a heavy cow-skin always by her side, and scarce an hour passed during the day but was marked by the blood of one of these slaves. The girls seldom passed her without her saying, "Move faster, you *black gip!*"—continuing, "If you don't move faster, I'll move you!" Added to the cruel lashings to which these slaves were subjected, they were kept nearly half starved. They seldom knew what it was to eat a full meal. I have seen Mary contending with the pigs for the offal thrown into the street. So much was Mary kicked and cut to pieces, that she was oftener called "*pecked*" than by her name.

I lived in Master Hugh's family about seven years. During this time, I succeeded in learning to read and write. In accomplishing this, I was compelled to resort to various stratagems. I had no regular teacher. My mistress, who had kindly commenced to instruct me, had, in compliance with the advice and direction of her husband, not only ceased to instruct, but had set her face against my being instructed by any one else. It is due, however, to my mistress to say of her, that she did not adopt this course of treatment immediately. She at first lacked the depravity indispensable to shutting me up in mental darkness. It was at least necessary for her to have some training in the exercise of irresponsible power, to make her equal to the task of treating me as though I were a brute.

My mistress was, as I have said, a kind and tender-hearted woman; and in the simplicity of her soul she commenced, when I first went to live with her, to treat me as she supposed one human being ought to treat another. In entering upon the duties of a slaveholder, she did not seem to perceive that I sustained to her the relation of a mere chattel, and that for her to treat me as a human being was not only wrong, but dangerously so. Slavery proved as injurious to her as it did to me. When I went there, she was a pious, warm, and tenderhearted woman. There was no sorrow or suffering for which she had not a tear. She had bread for the hungry, clothes for the naked, and comfort for every mourner that came within her reach. Slavery soon proved its ability to divest her of these heavenly qualities. Under its influence, the tender heart became stone, and the lamblike disposition gave way to one of tiger-like fierceness. The first step in her downward course, was in her ceasing to instruct me. She now commenced to practice her husband's precepts. She finally became even more violent in her opposition than her husband himself. She was not satisfied with simply doing as well as he had commanded; she seemed anxious to do better. Nothing seemed to make her more angry than to see me with a newspaper. She seemed to think that here lay the danger. I have had her rush at me with a face made all up of fury, and snatch from me a newspaper, in a manner that fully revealed her apprehension. She was an apt woman; and a little experience soon demonstrated, to her satisfaction, that education and slavery were incompatible with each other.

From this time I was most narrowly watched. If I was in a separate room any considerable length of time, I was sure to be suspected of having a book, and was at once called to give an account of myself. All this, however, was too late. The first step had been taken. Mistress, in teaching me the alphabet, had given me the *inch*, and no precaution could prevent me from taking the *ell*.

The plan which I adopted, and the one by which I was most successful, was that of making friends of all the little white boys whom I met in the street. As many of these as I could, I converted into teachers. With their kindly aid, obtained at different times and in different places, I finally succeeded in learning to read. When I was sent off on errands, I always took my book with me, and by going one part of my errand quickly, I found time to get a lesson before my return. I used also to carry bread with me, enough of which was always in the house, and to which I was always welcome; for I was much better off in this regard than many of the poor white children in our neighborhood. This bread I used to bestow upon the hungry little urchins, who, in return, would give me that more valuable bread of knowledge. I am strongly tempted to give the names of two or three of those little boys, as a testimonial of the gratitude and affection I bear them; but prudence forbids—not that it would injure me, but it might embarrass them; for it is almost an unpardonable offense to teach slaves to read in this Christian country. It is enough to say of the dear little fellows, that they lived on Philpot Street, very near Durgin and Bailey's ship-yard. I used to talk this matter of slavery over with them. I would sometimes say to them, I wished I could be as free as they would be when they got to be men. "You will be free as soon as you are twenty-one, *but I am a slave for life!* Have not I as good a right to be free as you have?" These words used to trouble them; they would express for me the liveliest sympathy, and console me with the hope that something would occur by which I might be free.

3

FROM

Up from Slavery

by Booker T. Washington

(1858?–1915)

Booker T. Washington was born in a Virginia slave cabin in 1858 or 1859. Although he was very young at the time of the Emancipation Proclamation, he vividly recalls his early days as a plantation slave.

Washington was an extraordinary individual by any standards, but that he achieved as much as he did with such truly humble beginnings is a remarkable feat. Washington's story is interesting on two counts: first, for its descriptions of the life of a slave boy on a Southern plantation, and second, for its exciting narration of his adventures in securing an education. Upon reading of the hardships that Washington willingly endured to obtain his education, we must reflect upon the almost unerring certainty with which an ambitious mind will seize upon education as the key to success and power.

Washington went on to international fame as the founder of Tuskegee Institute, a school for Negroes which emphasized industrial training. By the turn of the century he was one of the most influential educators and racial advisors on the American scene.

This enlightening selection is a tribute not only to its author, but also to the inquiring nature of man himself.

I WAS born a slave on a plantation in Franklin County, Virginia. I am not quite sure of the exact place or exact date of my birth, but at any rate I suspect I must have been born somewhere and at some time. As nearly as I have been able to learn, I was born near a cross-roads post-office called Hale's Ford, and the year was 1858 or 1859. I do not know the month or the day. The earliest impressions I can now recall are of the plantation and the slave quarters—the latter being the part of the plantation where the slaves had their cabins.

My life had its beginning in the midst of the most miserable, desolate, and discouraging surroundings. This was so, however, not because my owners were especially cruel, for they were not, as compared with many others. I was born in a typical log cabin, about fourteen by sixteen feet square. In this cabin I lived with my mother and a brother and sister till after the Civil War, when we were all declared free.

Of my ancestry I know almost nothing. In the slave quarters, and even later, I heard whispered conversations among the coloured people of the tortures which the slaves, including, no doubt, my ancestors on my mother's side, suffered in the middle passage of the slave ship while being conveyed from Africa to America. I have been unsuccessful in securing any information that would throw any accurate light upon the history of my family beyond my mother. She, I remember, had a half-brother and a half-sister. In the days of slavery not very much attention was given to family history and family records —that is, black family records. My mother, I suppose, attracted the attention of a purchaser who was afterward my owner and hers. Her addition to the slave family attracted about as much attention as the purchase of a new horse or cow. Of my father I know even less than of my mother. I do not even know his name. I have heard reports to the effect that he was a white man who lived on one of the near-by plantations. Whoever he was, I never heard of his taking the least interest in me or providing in any way for my rearing. But I do not find especial fault with him. He was simply another unfortunate victim of the institution which the Nation unhappily had engrafted upon it at that time.

The cabin was not only our living place, but was also used as the kitchen for the plantation. My mother was the plantation cook. The cabin was without glass windows; it had only openings in the side which let in the light, and also the cold, chilly air of winter. There was a door to the cabin—that is, something that was called a door— but the uncertain hinges by which it was hung, and the large cracks in it, to say nothing of the fact that it was too small, made the room a very uncomfortable one. In addition to those openings there was, in the lower right-hand corner of the room, the "cat hole,"—a contrivance which almost every mansion or cabin in Virginia possessed during the ante-bellum period. The "cat hole" was a square opening, about seven by eight inches provided for the purpose of letting the cat pass in and out of the house at will during the night. In the case of our particular cabin I could never understand the necessity for this convenience, since there were at least a dozen or half dozen other places in the cabin that would have accommodated the cats. There was no wooden floor in our cabin, the naked earth being used as a floor. In the center of the earthen floor there was a large, deep opening covered with boards, which was used as a place in which to store sweet potatoes, during the winter. An impression of this potato-hole is very distinctly engraved upon my memory, because I recall that during the process of putting the potatoes in or taking them out I would often come into possession of one or two, which I roasted and thoroughly enjoyed. There was no cooking-stove on our plantation, and all the cooking for the whites and slaves my mother had to do over an open fireplace, mostly in pots and "skillits." While the poorly built cabin caused us to suffer with cold in the winter, the heat from the open fireplace in summer was equally trying.

The early years of my life, which were spent in the little cabin, were not very different from those of thousands of other slaves. My mother, of course, had little time in which to give attention to the training of her children during the day. She snatched a few moments for our care in the early morning before her work began, and at night after the day's work was done. One of my earliest recollections is that of my mother cooking a chicken late at night, and awakening the children for the purpose of feeding them. How or where she got it I do not know. I presume, however, it was procured from our owner's farm. Some people may call this theft. If such a thing were to happen now, I should condemn it as theft myself. But taking place at the time it did, and for the reason that it did, no one could ever make me believe that my mother was guilty of thieving. She was simply a victim of the system of slavery. I cannot remember having slept in a bed until after our family was declared free by the Emancipation Proclamation. Three children—John, my older brother, Amanda, my sister, and myself—had a pallet on the dirt floor, or, to be more correct, we slept in and on a bundle of filthy rags laid upon the dirt floor.

I was asked not long ago to tell something about the sports and pastimes that I engaged in during my youth. Until that question was asked it had never occurred to me that there was no period of my life that was devoted to play. From the time that I can remember anything, almost every day of my life has been occupied in some kind of labour; though I think I would now be a more useful man if I had had time for sports. During the period that I spent in slavery I was not large enough to be of much service, still I was occupied most of the time in cleaning the yards, carrying water to men in the fields, or going to the mill to which I used to take the corn, once a week, to be ground. The mill was about three miles from the plantation. This work I always dreaded. The heavy bag of corn would be thrown across the back of the horse, and the corn divided about evenly on each side; but in some way, almost without exception, on these trips, the corn would shift as to become unbalanced and would fall off the horse, and often I would fall with it. As I was not strong enough to reload the corn upon the horse, I would have to wait, sometimes for many hours, till a chance passer-by came along who would help me out of my trouble. The hours while waiting for some one were usually spent in crying. The time consumed in this way made me late in reaching the mill, and by the time I got my corn ground and reached home it would be far into the night. The road was a lonely one, and often led through dense forests. I was always frightened. The woods were said to be full of soldiers who had deserted from the army, and I had been told that the first thing a deserter did to a Negro boy when he found him alone was to cut off his ears. Besides, when I was late in getting home I knew I would always get a severe scolding or a flogging.

I had no schooling whatever while I was a slave, though I remember on several occasions I went as far as the schoolhouse door with one of my young mistresses to carry her books. The picture of several dozen boys and girls in a schoolroom engaged in study made a deep impression upon me, and I had the feeling that to get into a schoolhouse and study in this way would be about the same as getting into paradise.

So far as I can now recall, the first knowledge that I

got of the fact that we were slaves, and that freedom of the slaves was being discussed, was early one morning before day, when I was awakened by my mother kneeling over her children and fervently praying that Lincoln and his armies might be successful, and that one day she and her children might be free. In this connection I have never been able to understand how the slaves throughout the South, completely ignorant as were the masses so far as books or newspapers were concerned, were able to keep themselves so accurately and completely informed about the great National questions that were agitating the country. From the time that Garrison, Lovejoy, and others began to agitate for freedom, the slaves throughout the South kept in close touch with the progress of the movement. Though I was a mere child during the preparation for the Civil War and during the war itself, I now recall the many late-at-night whispered discussions that I heard my mother and the other slaves on the plantation indulge in. These discussions showed that they understood the situation, and that they kept themselves informed of events by what was termed the "grape-vine" telegraph.

During the campaign when Lincoln was first a candidate for the Presidency, the slaves on our far-off plantation, miles from any railroad or large city or daily newspaper, knew what the issues involved were. When war was begun between the North and the South, every slave on our plantation felt and knew that, though other issues were discussed, the primal one was that of slavery. Even the most ignorant members of my race on the remote plantations felt in their hearts, with a certainty that admitted of no doubt, that the freedom of the slaves would be the one great result of the war, if the Northern armies conquered. Every success of the Federal armies and every defeat of the Confederate forces was watched with the keenest and most intense interest. Often the slaves got knowledge of the results of great battles before the white people at the "big house," as the master's house was called.

I cannot remember a single instance during my childhood or early boyhood when our entire family sat down to the table together, and God's blessing was asked, and the family ate a meal in a civilized manner. On the plantation in Virginia, and even later, meals were gotten by the children very much as dumb animals get theirs. It was a piece of bread here and a scrap of meat there. It was a cup of milk at one time and some potatoes at another. Sometimes a portion of our family would eat out of the skillet or pot, while some one would eat from a tin plate held on the knees, and often using nothing but the hands with which to hold the food. When I had grown to sufficient size, I was required to go to the "big house" at meal-times to fan the flies from the table by means of a large set of paper fans operated by a pulley. Naturally much of the conversation of the white people turned upon the subject of freedom and the war, and I absorbed a good deal of it. I remember that at one time I saw two of my young mistresses and some lady visitors eating ginger-cakes in the yard. At that time those cakes seemed to me to be absolutely the most tempting and desirable things that I had ever seen; and I then and there resolved that, if I ever got free, the height of my ambition would be reached if I could get to the point where I could secure and eat ginger-cakes in the way that I saw those ladies doing.

Of course as the war was prolonged the white people, in many cases, often found it difficult to secure food for themselves. I think the slaves felt the deprivation less than the white, because the usual diet for the slaves was corn bread and pork, and these could be raised on the plantation; but coffee, tea, sugar, and other articles which the whites had been accustomed to use could not be raised on the plantation, and the conditions brought about by the war frequently made it impossible to secure these things. The whites were often in great straits. Parched corn was used for coffee, and a kind of black molasses was used instead of sugar. Many times nothing was used to sweeten the so-called tea and coffee.

The first pair of shoes I recall wearing were wooden ones. They had rough leather on the top, but the bottoms, which were about an inch thick, were of wood. When I walked they made a fearful noise, and besides this they were very inconvenient, since there was no yielding to the natural pressure of the foot.

In wearing them one presented an exceedingly awkward appearance. The most trying ordeal that I was forced to endure as a slave boy, however, was the wearing of a flax shirt. In the portion of Virginia where I lived it was common to use flax as a part of the clothing for the slaves. That part of the flax from which our clothing was made was largely the refuse, which of course was the cheapest and roughest part. I can scarcely imagine any torture, except perhaps, the pulling of a tooth, that is equal to that caused by putting on a new flax shirt for the first time. It is almost equal to the feeling that one would experience if he had a dozen or more chestnut burrs, or a hundred small pinpoints, in contact with his flesh. Even to this day I can recall accurately the tortures that I underwent when putting on one of these garments. The fact that my flesh was soft and tender added to the pain. But I had no choice. I had to wear the flax shirt or none; and had it been left to me to choose, I should have chosen to wear no covering. In connection with the flax shirt, my brother John, who is several years older than I am, performed one of the most generous acts that I ever heard of one slave relative doing for another. On several occasions when I was being forced to wear a new flax shirt, he generously agreed to put it on in my stead and wear it for several days, till it was "broken in." Until I had grown to be quite a youth this single garment was all that I wore.

My mother's husband, who was the stepfather of my brother John and myself, did not belong to the same owners as did my mother. In fact, he seldom came to our plantation. I remember seeing him there perhaps once a year, that being about Christmas time. In some way, during the war, by running away and following the Federal soldiers, it seems, he found his way into the new state of West Virginia. As soon as freedom was declared, he sent for my mother to come to the Kanawha Valley, in West Virginia. At that time a journey from Virginia over the mountains to West Virginia was rather a tedious and in some cases a painful undertaking. What little clothing and few household goods we had were placed in a cart, but the children walked the greater portion of the distance, which was several hundred miles.

I do not think any of us ever had been very far from the plantation, and the taking of a long journey into another state was quite an event. The parting from our former owners and the members of our own race on the plantation was a serious occasion. From the time of our parting till their death we kept up a correspondence with the older members of the family, and in later years we have kept in touch with those who were the younger members. We were several weeks making the trip, and most of the time we slept in the open air and did our cooking over a log fire out of doors. One night I recall that we camped near an abandoned log cabin, and my mother decided to build a fire in that for cooking, and afterward to make a "pallet" on the floor for our sleeping. Just as the fire had gotten well started a large black snake fully a yard and a half long dropped down the chimney and ran out on the floor. Of course we at once abandoned that cabin. Finally we reached our destination—a little town called Malden, which is about five miles from Charleston, the present capital of the state.

At that time salt-mining was the great industry in that part of West Virginia, and the little town of Malden was right in the midst of the salt-furnaces. My stepfather had already secured a job at the salt-furnace and he had also secured a little cabin for us to live in. Our new house was no better than the one we had left on the old plantation in Virginia. In fact, in one respect it was worse. Notwithstanding the poor condition of our plantation cabin, we were at all times sure of pure air. Our new home was in the midst of a cluster of cabins crowded closely together, and as there were no sanitary regulations, the filth about the cabins was often intolerable. Some of our neighbors were coloured people, and some were the poorest and most ignorant and degraded white people. It was a motley mixture. Drinking, gambling, quarrels, fights, and shockingly immoral practices were frequent. All who lived in the little town were in one way or another connected with the salt business. Though I was a mere child, my stepfather put me and my brother at work in one of the furnaces. Often I began work as early as four o'clock in the morning.

The first thing I ever learned in the way of book knowledge was while working in the salt-furnace. Each salt-packer had his barrels marked with a certain number. The number allotted to my stepfather was "18." At the close of the day's work the boss of the packers would come around and put "18" on each of our barrels, and I soon learned to recognize that figure whenever I saw it, and after a while got to the point where I could make that figure, though I knew nothing about any other figures or letters.

From the time that I can remember having any thoughts about anything, I recall that I had an intense longing to learn to read. I determined, when quite a small child, that, if I accomplished nothing else in life, I would in some way get enough education to enable me to read common books and newspapers. Soon after we got settled in some manner in our new cabin in West Virginia, I induced my mother to get hold of a book for me. How or where she got it I do not know, but in some way she procured an old copy of Webster's "blueback" spelling-book, which contained the alphabet, followed by such meaningless words as "ab," "ba," "ca," "da." I began at once to devour this book, and I think that it was the first one I have had in my hands. I had learned from somebody that the way to begin to read was to learn the alphabet, so I tried in all the ways I could think of to learn it—all of course without a teacher, for I could find no one to teach me. At that time there was not a single member of my race anywhere near us who could read, and I was too timid to approach any of the white people. In some way, within a few weeks, I mastered the greater portion of the alphabet. In all my efforts to learn to read my mother shared fully my ambition, and sympathized with me and aided me in every way that she could. Though she was totally ignorant, so far as mere book knowledge was concerned, she had high ambitions for her children, and a large fund of good, hard, common sense which seemed to enable her to meet and master every situation. If I have done anything in life worth attention, I feel sure that I inherited the disposition from my mother.

In the midst of my struggles and longing for an education, a young coloured boy who had learned to read in the state of Ohio came to Malden. As soon as the coloured people found out that he could read, a newspaper was secured, and at the close of nearly every day's work this young man would be surrounded by a group of men and women who were anxious to hear him read the news contained in the papers. How I used to envy this man! He seemed to me to be the one young man in all the world who ought to be satisfied with his attainments.

About this time the question of having some kind of a school opened for the coloured children in the village began to be discussed by members of the race. As it would be the first school for Negro children that had ever been opened in that part of Virginia, it was, of course, to be a great event, and the discussion excited the wildest interest. The most perplexing question was where to find a teacher. The young man from Ohio who had learned to read the papers was considered, but his age was against him. In the midst of the discussion about a teacher, another young coloured man from Ohio, who had been a soldier, in some way found his way into town. It was soon learned that he possessed considerable education, and he was engaged by the coloured people to teach their first school. As yet no free schools had been started for coloured people in that section, hence each family agreed to pay a certain amount per month, with the understanding that the teacher was to "board 'round"—that is, spend a day with each family. This was not bad for the teacher, for each family tried to provide the very best on the day the teacher was to be its guest. I recall that I looked forward with anxious appetite to the "teacher's day" at our little cabin.

This experience of a whole race beginning to go to school for the first time, presents one of the most interesting studies that has ever occurred in connection with the development of any race. Few people who were not right in the midst of the scenes can form any exact idea of the intense desire which the people of my race showed for an education. As I have stated, it was a whole race trying to go to school. Few were too young, and none too old, to make the attempt to learn. As fast as any kind of teachers could be secured, not only were day-schools filled, but night-schools as well. The great ambition of the older people was to try to learn to read the Bible before they died. With this end in view, men and women who were fifty or seventy-five years old would often be found in the night-school. Sunday-schools were formed soon after freedom, but the principal book studied in the Sunday-school was the spelling-book. Day-school, night-school, Sunday-school, were always crowded, and often many had to be turned away for want of room.

The opening of the school in the Kanawha Valley, however, brought to me one of the keenest disappointments that I ever experienced. I had been working in a salt-furnace for several months, and my stepfather had discovered that I had a financial value, and so, when the school opened, he decided that he would not spare me from my work. This decision seemed to cloud my every ambition. The disappointment was made all the more severe by reason of the fact that my place of work was where I could see the happy children passing to and from school, mornings and afternoons. Despite this disappointment, however, I determined that I would learn something, anyway. I applied myself with greater earnestness than ever to the mastering of what was in the "blue-back" speller.

My mother sympathized with me in my disappointment, and sought to comfort me in all the ways she could, and to help me find a way to learn. After a while I succeeded in making arrangements with the teacher to give me some lessons at night, after the day's work was done. These night lessons were so welcome that I think I learned more at night than the other children did during the day. My own experiences in the night-school gave me faith in the night-school idea, with which, in after years, I had to do both at Hampton and Tuskegee. But my boyish heart was still set upon going to day-school, and I let no opportunity slip to push my case. Finally, I won, and was permitted to go to the school in the day for a few months, with the understanding that I was to rise early in the morning and work in the furnace till nine o'clock, and return immediately after school closed in the afternoon for at least two more hours of work.

The schoolhouse was some distance from the furnace, and as I had to work till nine o'clock, and the school opened at nine, I found myself in a difficulty. School would always be begun before I reached it, and sometimes my class had recited. To get around this difficulty I yielded to a temptation for which most people, I suppose, will condemn me; but since it is a fact, I might as well state it. I have great faith in the power and influence of facts. It is seldom that anything is permanently gained by holding back a fact. There was a large clock in a little office in the furnace. This clock, of course, all the hundred or more workmen depended upon to regulate their hours of beginning and ending their day's work. I got the idea that the way for me to reach school on time was to move the clock hands from half-past eight up to the nine o'clock mark. This I found myself doing morning after morning, till the furnace "boss" discovered that something was wrong, and locked the clock in a case. I did not mean to inconvenience anybody. I simply meant to reach that schoolhouse in time.

When, however, I found myself at the school for the first time, I also found myself confronted with two other difficulties. In the first place, I found that all of the other children wore hats or caps on their heads, and I had neither hat nor cap. In fact, I do not remember that up to the time of going to school I had ever worn any kind of covering upon my head, nor do I recall that either I or anybody else had even thought anything about the need of covering for my head. But, of course, when I saw how all the other boys were dressed, I began to feel quite uncomfortable. As usual, I put the case before my mother, and she explained to me that she had no money with which to buy a "store hat," which was a rather new institution at that time among the members of my race and was considered quite the thing for young and old to own, but that she would find a way to help me out of the difficulty. She accordingly got two pieces of "homespun" (jeans) and sewed them together, and I was soon the proud possessor of my first cap.

The lesson that my mother taught me in this has always remained with me, and I have tried as best I could to teach it to others. I have always felt proud, whenever I think of the incident, that my mother had the strength of character enough not to be led into the temptation of seeming to be that which she was not—of trying to impress my schoolmates and others with the fact that she was able to buy me a "store hat" when she was not. I have always felt proud that she refused to go into debt for that which she did not have the money to pay for. Since that time I have owned many kinds of caps and hats, but never one of which I have felt so proud as of the cap made of the two pieces of cloth sewed together by my mother. I have noted the fact, but without satisfaction, I need not add, that several of the boys who began their careers with "store hats" and who were my schoolmates and used to join in the sport that was made of me because I had only a "homespun" cap, have ended their careers in the penitentiary, while others are not able now to buy any kind of hat.

My second difficulty was with regard to my name, or rather *a* name. From the time when I could remember anything, I had been called simply "Booker." Before going to school it had never occurred to me that it was needful or appropriate to have an additional name. When I heard the school-roll called, I noticed that all of the children had at least two names, and some of them indulged in what seemed to me the extravagance of having three. I was in deep perplexity, because I knew that the teacher would demand of me at least two names, and I had only one. By the time the occasion came for the enrolling of my name, an idea occurred to me which I thought would make me equal to the situation; and so, when the teacher asked me what my full name was, I calmly told him "Booker Washington," as if I had been called by that name all my life; and by that name I have since been known. Later in life I found that my mother had given me the name of "Booker Taliaferro" soon after I was born, but in some way that part of my name seemed to disappear, and for a long while was forgotten, but as soon as I found out about it I revived it and made my full name "Booker Taliaferro Washington." I think there are not many men in our country who have had the privilege of naming themselves in the way that I have.

More than once I have tried to picture myself in the position of a boy or man with an honoured and distinguished ancestry which I could trace back through a period of hundreds of years, and who had not only inherited a name, but fortune and a proud family homestead; and yet I have sometimes had the feeling that if I had inherited these, and had been a member of a more popular race, I should have been inclined to yield to the temptation of depending upon my ancestry and my colour to do that for me which I should do for myself. Years ago I resolved that because I had no ancestry myself I would leave a record of which my children would be proud, and which might encourage them to still higher effort.

The world should not pass judgement upon the Negro, and especially the Negro youth, too quickly or too harshly. The Negro boy has obstacles, discouragements, and temptations to battle with that are little known to those not situated as he is. When a white boy undertakes a task, it is taken for granted that he will succeed. On the other hand, people are usually surprised if the Negro boy does not fail. In a word, the Negro youth starts out with the presumption against him.

The influence of ancestry, however, is important in helping forward any individual or race, if too much reliance is not placed upon it. Those who constantly direct attention to the Negro youth's moral weaknesses, and compare his advancement with that of white youth, do not consider the influence of the memories which cling about the old family homesteads. I have no idea, as I have stated elsewhere, who my grandmother was. I have, or have had uncles and aunts and cousins, but I have no knowledge as to what most of them are. My case will illustrate that of hundreds of thousands of black people in every part of our country. The very fact that the white boy is conscious that, if he fails in life, he will disgrace the whole family record, extending back through many generations, is of tremendous value in helping him to resist temptations. The fact that the individual has behind and surrounding him proud family history and connection serves as a stimulus to help him to overcome obstacles when striving for success.

The time that I was permitted to attend school during the day was short, and my attendance was irregular. It was not long before I had to stop attending day-school altogether, and devote all of my time again to work. I resorted to the night-school again. In fact, the greater part of the education I secured in my boyhood was gathered through the night-school after my day's work was done. I had difficulty often in securing a satisfactory teacher. Sometimes, after I had secured some one to teach me at night, I would find, much to my disappointment, that the teacher knew little more than I did. Often I would have to walk several miles at night in order to recite my night-school lessons. There was never a time in my youth, no matter how dark and discouraging the days might be, when one resolve did not continually remain with me, and that was a determination to secure an education at any cost. . . .

4

FROM

The Black Man's Burden

by William H. Holtzclaw

(1870?–1943)

The emancipation of the slaves was the culmination of many years of hope and prayer for the Negroes, but they were soon to discover that the mere fact of freedom did not improve their lot to any significant degree. The only trade familiar to many slaves was farming, and the only way they could continue to farm after the Civil War was under some form of sharecropping system. The result was generally substitution of economic slavery for their former plight. It was a rugged struggle which many did not survive.

William Holtzclaw was born toward the end of the Reconstruction era in the Deep South, and later in life recalled quite clearly the hardships under the sharecrop system. After completing his own education with much difficulty, he tried to enlighten the Alabama community in which he lived by publishing a newspaper for Negroes. Not satisfied with the results of this effort, he was determined to start a school for people of his own race, and did so in the early days of the new century. By 1915 Holtzclaw's school, the Utica Normal and Industrial In-

stitute in Utica, Mississippi, could boast an enrollment of five hundred students.

I HAVE some recollection of the house in which I was born, and of the great plantation which belonged, in the days of slavery, to one of those traditional Southern planters about whom we have read so much. I have seen the windowless house in which I first saw the light—the light that scantily streamed through the cracks in the wall. It was a little cabin, fourteen feet by sixteen feet, made of split pine poles, with only dirt for a floor.

It was in this cabin, near Roanoke, Randolf County, Alabama, that my mother was left alone one Saturday night. My father had gone away to secure food for her, and when he returned, Sunday morning, I was there to greet him. My mother and I were completely alone at the time of my birth.

I have always felt that I have an advantage over most men of my race in that I was born on a day of rest, It was the first piece of good fortune that came to me, and I want to be grateful for it.

This was in the closing days of Reconstruction, when there were stirring times in nearly every part of the country, but of course, I do not remember much about what happened then. I recall, however, some things that occurred four or five years later, when, although the South had been legally reconstructed, the law had not changed the sentiments of the people very much.

I distinctly remember that there were no colored school-teachers at that time and, in my own locality, there were no Northern white teachers. The few colored schools that existed at all were taught by Southern white men and women. Before I was old enough to attend school myself I used to go along now and then with the others, and I remember that one of these Southern white teachers took a great liking to me and, passing our house one day on his way home, predicted to my mother that I would some day be a lawyer. I did not know what that meant then, but I got the impression that it meant I was going to be something great, and I did not forget it.

Almost as soon as the Negro pupils got as far as "baker," and certainly when they got as far as "abasement," in the old blue-back speller, they were made assistant teachers, and in a short while, relieving the white teachers, they became the only teachers we had. When I was seven years old there was not a white teacher in our community. The colored teachers were doing pretty good work, but the best of them had advanced only about as far as the fourth grade. There is one thing, however, that they had learned to perfection, and that was the use of the rod, and of this kind of education I got my full share every day. My great trouble was that if I got a whipping at school, I was likely to get another one when I got home.

This was not always the case, however. One year it had been agreed that I should study nothing but arithmetic, and before I had been at school many days, I had undoubtedly reached the limit of my teacher's ability in that branch. For several days I had no lessons. At length, one day, without warning, he jumped at me like a fierce tiger, and with a hickory switch, which he had previously roasted in the fire, beat me to the floor and continued to flog me until some grown pupils interfered. When I started home that afternoon I became exhausted and sat down on a log on the roadside, from which I was not able to rise on account of the lacerated condition of my flesh. My father found me after dark and carried me home. That was the only time that I can now recall ever having seen my father very angry. He wanted to whip that school-teacher, but my mother's advice prevailed, and I was sent back to school as soon as I could walk. Those early experiences made me vow that if ever I got to be a school-teacher I would not whip the little ones and let the big ones go free.

My father—who, like my mother, had been a slave—was a young and inexperienced man when he married. My mother, however, had been married twice before, and she was the mother of three children. Her first marriage was performed in slavery time by the simple act of jumping back and forth over a broom in the presence of her master and mistress. In the course of time as more children, including myself, came along, until there were six of us, my father found it very difficult to keep the wolf from the door.

My mother helped him by cooking for the landlord's family, while my father worked on the plantation. Our landlord—one of those Southern planters, now commonly referred to as a "gentleman of the Old South"—like many others of his class, had had his fortune, consisting largely of slaves, swept away by the ravages of the Civil War. The result was that, although he had a large amount of land left, he was nevertheless a poor man. The agreement between him and Father, which was nothing more than a verbal contract between them, provided that he was to furnish land, mules, seed—in fact, everything but labor—and further provided that he was to help do the work and receive as his share three-fourths of all that the land produced, while we were to receive the other one-fourth.

Although he agreed to help, he seldom did any manual labor. He was in the fields every day, however, going from place to place among the various Negroes that were serving under contracts similar to ours. At one time my father ventured, in the most modest way, to call his attention to the fact that he was doing no work, but he very kindly, yet firmly, explained that he was doing more work in a day without a tool in his hand than my father was doing in a month. He tried to make my father understand this. I do not know whether my father understood it or not, but I could not.

We never prepared our land for cultivation, but simply

planted the seeds on the hard ground in March and April and covered them with a turn plow; then we cultivated the crop for two months. Naturally, the returns were small. When the crop was divided in the fall of the year three loads of corn were thrown into the white man's crib and one into ours; but when it came to dividing the cotton, which was done up into bales weighing five hundred pounds each and which sold for seventeen cents a pound, every bale went to the white man. He was at great pains to explain to my father each year that we ate ours during the year.

I remember how puzzled I used to be trying to conceive how it was possible for people to eat a crop—especially cotton out of which cloth is made—before it was produced. In later years, however, and many times since then, I have seen whole crops eaten two or three years before they were planted.

Our landlord furnished us food from his smoke-house from March to July, and from September to December. This food consisted of corn meal, out of which we made corn-pone by mixing it with water and salt, and smoked sides of meat, from hogs that we raised. All the rest of the time we had to find something to do away from the plantation in order to keep supplied with bread and clothes, which were scanty enough to support all the people that lived on it, even if it had been under better cultivation.

Each year the landlord would "run" us, and he would charge from twenty-five to two hundred per cent for the advances, according to the time of the year. No wonder we ate our crops up.

The method of obtaining food and provisions on this plantation was interesting. The landlord owned the store—one large room about forty feet by sixty feet, which he kept well supplied with flour, meat, meal, and tobacco. This store was usually open only on Saturdays, when all the Negroes from the plantation would come up and pass the day in the store, which was a sort of "social center." Meantime their rations for the following week were being issued. For an unmarried male laborer the usual ration was a pound of meat, a peck of meal, three pounds of flour, and a plug of tobacco.

I remember hearing the men complain very often that they were charged for rations that they did not get, and I remember that at one time a lawsuit arose between the landlord and a Negro on the plantation who could neither read nor write. When the trial came off at the store the landlord presented his books to show that the Negro had obtained certain rations during the year. The Negro denied having received such rations, and as proof he presented his "book," which consisted of a stick, one yard long, trimmed in hexagon fashion and filled with notches, each notch representing some purchase and in some ingenious way the time of the purchase. After the jury had examined the white man's books they began an examination of the Negro's stick, and the more he explained his way of keeping books, the more interested the jurors became. When the trial was over, the Negro won the case, the jurors having decided that he had kept his books properly and that a mistake had been made by the white bookkeeper.

My mother cooked for the "white folks," and, her work being very exacting, she could not always get home at night. At such times we children suffered an excruciating kind of pain—the pain of hunger. I can well remember how at night we would often cry for food until falling here and there on the floor we would sob ourselves to sleep. Late at night, sometimes after midnight, mother would reach home with a large pan of pot-liquor, or more often a variety of scraps from the "white folks'" table (she might have brought more, but she was not the kind of cook that slipped things out of the back door); waking us all, she would place the pan on the floor, or on her knees, and gathering around we would eat to our satisfaction.

There was neither knife, fork nor spoon—nothing but the pan. We used our hands and sometimes in our haste dived head foremost into the pan, very much as pigs after swill. In the morning, when mother had to return to her work before we children awoke, she was accustomed to put the large pan on the dirt floor in the middle of the cabin where we could find it without difficulty. Sometimes, however, our pet pig would come in and find it first, and would be already helping himself before we could reach it. We never made any serious objection to dividing with him, and I do not recall that he showed any resentment about dividing with us.

One day my brother and I were given a meal of pie-crust, which my mother had brought from the "white folks'" table. As we were eating it, Old Buck, the family dog, who resembled an emaciated panther, stole one of the crusts. We loved Old Buck, but we had to live, and so my brother "lit onto" him and a royal battle took place over that crust. As my brother was losing ground, I joined in the struggle. We saved the crust, but not until both of us had been scratched and bitten. I do not know who needed the crust most, we or the dog, for those were the days of hardships. Very often we would go two or three days at a time without prepared food, but we usually found our way into the potato patches, and the chickens were not always safe where we passed, for my brother occasionally, by accident, would step on a little one, and of course we would then have to cook it as a matter of economy. I recall that in that section of Alabama where I lived there is a kind of root called hog potato, which grows abundantly in the swamps and marshy places. I have never known it by any other name. I used to spend hours every day in the swamps about our house wading in the slush above my knees, turning up the mud in search of those potatoes. After they were roasted they had a taste like that of the white potato with which people in the Northern states are familiar. By means of these potatoes, together with berries and other wild fruits, we were able to keep body and soul together during those dark days.

As I now remember it, my father's continuous effort was to keep the wolf from the door. He presently quit the big plantation and spent a year working on the Western railway of Alabama, at Loachapoka in Lee county, about fifty miles from home. There were no railroads or stage coaches to carry him to and from his work, so it required two weeks to make the round trip, much of which lay through immense forests where a narrow footpath was the only passage. He would remain away from home three months at a time, working for the handsome sum of a dollar a day, out of which he boarded himself and furnished his working-clothes. I remember how mother and we children would sit in our dark little cabin many nights looking for him to come at any moment, and sometimes it would be nearly a week after we would begin to look for him before he would come. I don't think we ever had a letter from him; we only knew that the three months were up, and that it was time for him to come to us.

He usually brought from forty to fifty dollars home, but by the time we paid out of that amount what we owed the white gentleman, on whose place we still lived, for the advances obtained of him in my father's absence there would not be much left for us.

The lack of food was not the only hardship we had to endure. We found it very difficult to find clothes and even shoes, which was very trying when the winters were cold. I never wore a pair of shoes until I was fifteen, and when I did begin to wear shoes I never wore them until the weather was cold. In fact, I made it a rule never to put on my new shoes until Christmas morning, no matter how cold it was. Usually in the summertime the only garment that we children wore was a simple shirt. These shirts were not always made of shirting, but were often of homespun, and when this material could not be had a crocus sack, or something of the kind, was used instead.

I remember that the first suit of clothes I owned I paid for myself with the money I had made by splitting rails. It took me a good part of the fall season to split the two thousand rails that were required to get my little suit, but I succeeded in my undertaking, with occasional help from my father in finishing the job. The fact that I bought this suit with my own labor made me think all the more of it.

Although the census taker of 1880 classed my parents as illiterates, they had a very clear understanding of right and wrong; in their own way they were moral teachers, and they knew how to make their lessons impressive. By no stretch of the imagination could either of them have been classed with what was known at that time as an ignorant Negro, though neither of them could read or write.

One day while I was alone in the "white folks' " kitchen, where I had accompanied my mother to her daily work, I spied a little round box on the shelf. It was a box of matches such as I have not seen in twenty years. Curious to see what a match-head was like, I pinched one without removing it from the box. An explosion was heard, and the box was blown off the shelf, to my consternation. With a switch my mother began to administer to a rather tender part of my anatomy the treatment with which it was already familiar, explaining all the while that I must learn to mind my own business. The white lady, with whom I was a favorite, interceded for me, saying that I should not be whipped for a little thing like that; it was most natural; I had reached the age of investigation. My mother desisted, shaking her head as she left the scene, saying she would "investigate" me, and from time to time she did. So in matters of conduct, at least, whether large or small, I had the advantage of a loving but firm discipline.

In such matters of conduct, or of morality, if you please, my mother was always teaching me some little lessons. I remember that at one time, when I must have been five or six years old, I was sent up to the "big house" to borrow some meal from the "white folks" for supper. On my way back, while climbing over an old-fashioned rail fence, I discovered, while pausing for a few minutes on the top rail, a hen's nest full of eggs. The bait was tempting. I was hungry and wanted the eggs. I had never heard anybody say anything about taking that which did not belong to you, but somehow I felt that it was wrong to take those eggs. I knew they belonged to the white lady up at the "big house." After thinking the matter over for nearly a half hour, I decided to compromise by taking only a few of them, so I got as many as my little pocket would hold and carried them home. Sidling up to my mother in a rather sheepish fashion, I showed them to her and told her that I had found them, which was the truth. I remember that my mother was amused, but she kept her face turned from me and proceeded to teach me another one of those little lessons, which stayed by me and supported me in after years.

She told me it was wrong to steal from the "white folks," that "white folks" thought all Negroes would steal, and that we must show them that we would not. She said she knew I did not steal them, but that it would look that way, and that I must show that I did not by taking them right back to the white lady and giving them to her. That was a great task. After having spent an hour in going a distance of 300 yards, I reached the white lady with the eggs and told her that I had found them. I have always suspected that my mother had been there and had seen the white lady before my arrival. At least, that is the way it appears now, as I look back on it, for the good lady gave me an old-fashioned lecture about stealing and told me that, whenever I wanted anything she had, I should come up and ask for it. Then she gave me two of the eggs. I was quite young at that time, as I have said before, but was not too young to learn, and that lesson and others like it remained with me.

When I was four years old I was put to work on the farm—that is, at such work as I could do, such as riding a deaf and blind mule while my brother held the plow. When I was six years old my four-year-old brother and I had to go two miles through a lonely forest every morning in order to carry my father's breakfast and dinner to a sawmill, where he was hauling logs for sixty cents a day. The white man, Frank Weathers, who employed a large number of hands, both Negroes and whites, was considered one of the best and most upright men in that section of the country.

In those days there were no public schools in that part of the country for the Negroes. Indeed, public schools for whites were just beginning to be established. This man set aside a little house in the neighborhood of the sawmill, employed a teacher, and urged all the Negroes to send their children to this school. Not a great many of them, however, took advantage of his generosity, for this was at the time when everybody seemed to think that the Negro's only hope was in politics.

But my father and mother had great faith in education, and they were determined that their children should have that blessing of which they themselves had been deprived.

Soon, however, Mr. Weathers had cut all the timber that he could get in that section, and he therefore moved his mills to another district. This left us without a school. But my father was not to be outdone. He called a meeting of the men in that community, and they agreed to build a schoolhouse themselves. They went to the forest and cut pine poles about eight inches in diameter, split them in halves, and carried them on their shoulders to a nice shady spot, and there erected a little schoolhouse. The benches were made of the same material, and there was no floor nor chimney. Some of the other boys' trousers suffered when they sat on the new pine benches, which exuded rosin, but I had an advantage of them in this respect, for I wore only a shirt. In fact, I never wore trousers until I got to be so large that the white neighbors complained of my insufficient clothes.

Those benches, I distinctly remember, were constructed for boys and girls larger than I was, and my feet were always about fourteen inches above the ground. In this manner I sat for hours at a time swinging my feet in an effort to balance myself on the pine bench. My feet often swelled, so that when I did get on the ground to recite I felt as if a thousand pins were sticking through them, and it was very difficult for me to stand. For this inability to stand I often got a good flogging, for I could not convince the teacher that I was not trying to "make believe."

School lasted two months in the year—through July and August. The house was three miles from our home, and we walked every day, my oldest sister carrying me astride her neck when my legs gave out. Sometimes we would have nothing more than an ear of roasted green corn in our baskets for dinner. Very often we had simply wild persimmons, or ripe fruit picked from our landlord's orchard, or nuts and muscadines from the forest. If we had meat, ten to one it was because "Old Buck" had caught a 'possum or a hare the night before. Many a night the dogs and I hunted all night in order to catch a 'possum for the next day's noon meal.

Although we were young, we were observant, and in this way we learned some things in that school—among them, that the teacher, who was a married man, had fallen in love with his assistant teacher. He was constantly "making eyes" at her. She evidently reciprocated his affection, for at the end of the school year they eloped, and there was a great stir in the community in consequence. The people met at the little schoolhouse and very nearly decided that they would have no more school, but my father was there and counselled them that we had all suffered enough already from the affair and that we ought not to punish ourselves further. I attended the meeting myself with my father and I remember that my sympathies were all with "Miss Deely." True, she had run away with the principal of the school and nobody knew where they were, but I could not see what right anybody had to interfere with her love affairs, and I ventured to tell my mother so. Mother did not argue the question, but sat down and took me across her lap and proceeded to correct my views on the subject. Then she put the matter to me in the form of a question. She asked me how would I like to have some nice little lady run away with my father and leave me there for her to take care of. That settled it with me. Miss Deely was forever afterward in the wrong.

At the end of the first school year there was a trying time in our family. On this occasion the teacher ordered all the pupils to appear dressed in white. We had no white clothes, nor many of any other sort, for that matter. Father and Mother discussed our predicament nearly all one night. Father said it was foolish to buy clothes which could be used only for that occasion. But my ever resourceful mother was still determined that her children should look as well on this important occasion as any of our neighbors. However, when we went to bed the night before the exhibition we still had no white clothes and no cloth from which to make them. Nevertheless, when we awoke the next morning, all three of us had beautiful white suits. It came about in this way: my mother had a beautiful white Sunday petticoat, which she had cut up and made into suits for us. As there is just so much cloth in a petticoat and no more, the stuff had to be cut close to cover all three of us children, and as the petticoat had been worn several times and was, therefore, likely to tear, we had to be very careful how we stooped in moving about the stage, lest there should be a general splitting and tearing, with consequences that we were afraid to imagine. At the exhibition the next night we said our little pieces, and I suppose we looked about as well as the others; at least, we thought so, and that was sufficient. One thing I am sure of—there was no mother there who was prouder of her children than ours. The thing that made her so pleased was the fact that my speech made such an impression that our white landlord lifted me off the stage when I had finished speaking and gave me a quarter of a dollar.

If there happened to be a school in the winter time, I had sometimes to go bare-footed and always with scant clothing. Our landlady was very kind in such cases. She would give me clothes that had already been worn by her sons, and in turn I would bring broom straw, from the sages, with which she made her brooms. In this way I usually got enough clothes to keep me warm.

So, with my mother's encouragement, I went to school in spite of my bare feet. Often the ground would be frozen, and often there would be snow. My feet would crack and bleed freely, but when I reached home Mother would have a tub full of hot water ready to plunge me into and thaw me out. Although this caused my feet and legs to swell, it usually got me into shape for school the next day.

I remember once, when I had helped "lay by" the crops at home and was ready to enter the little one-month school, it was decided that I could not go, because I had no hat. My mother told me that if I could catch a 'coon and cure the skin, she would make me a cap out of that material. That night I went far into the forest with my hounds, and finally located a 'coon. The 'coon was a mighty fighter, and when he had driven off all my dogs I saw that the only chance for me to get a cap was to whip the 'coon myself, so together with the dogs I went at him, and finally we conquered him. The next week I went to school wearing my new 'coon-skin cap.

Exertions of this kind, from time to time, strengthened my will and my body, and prepared me for more trying tests which were to come later.

As I grew older it became more and more difficult for me to go to school. When cotton first began to open—early in the fall—it brought a higher price than at any other time of the year. At this time the landlord wanted us all to stop school and pick cotton. But mother wanted me to remain in school, so, when the landlord came to the quarters early in the morning to stir up the cotton pickers, she used to outgeneral him by hiding me behind the skillets, ovens, and pots, throwing some old rags over me until he was gone. Then she would slip me off to school through the back way. I can see her now with her hands upon my shoulder, shoving me along through the woods and underbrush, in a roundabout way, keeping me all the time out of sight of the great plantation until we reached the point, a mile away from home, where we came to the public road. There my mother would bid me good-bye, whereupon she would return to the plantation and try to make up to the landlord for the work of us both in the field as cotton pickers.

But when I became too large to be conveniently hidden behind our few small pots I had to take my place on the farm. When I was nine years old I began to work as a regular fieldhand. My mother now devised another plan to keep me in school: I took turns with my brother at the plow and in school; one day I plowed and he went to school, the next day he plowed and I went to school; what he learned on his school day he taught me at night and I did the same for him. In this way we each got a month of schooling during the year, and with that month of schooling we also acquired the habit of studying at home. That we learned little enough may be seen from the following incident: I was ordered to get a United States history, and my father went to the store to get one, but the storekeeper, not having one, sold him a "Biography of Martin Luther" instead, without telling him the difference, so I carried the book to school and studied it for a long time, thinking that I was learning something about the United States. My teacher had neglected to tell me the name of the land I lived in.

It was hard enough for me to find a way to go to school. When it was not one obstacle, it was another. More than once I worked hard for eleven months in the year without receiving a single penny. Then, in order to enter school, I split rails at fifty cents a hundred during the month of December to get money with which to buy clothes.

When I reached the age where my school days were for the time at an end I was hired out to a white man for wages, in order to help support the family. Seeing that there was no chance for further schooling, I became morose, disheartened, and pulled away from all social life, except the monthly religious meetings at the little cabin church. Nevertheless, I gathered all the books I could find or borrow and hid them in the white man's barn, where I spent every bit of my spare time in trying to satisfy my desire for knowledge of the world of books. In this manner I spent all my Sundays. It was during this time that I came across the "Life of Ignatius Sancho," who was an educated black West Indian. It was the first thing in the way of a biography of a colored man that I had found, and I cannot express the inspiration I received from learning for the first time that a colored man could really make history.

It was in 1880 that my father finally despaired of getting ahead by working on the share system—that is, by working crops for half the profit. Encouraged by the success of other Negroes around him and urged on by the determination of my mother and the persistence of us children, he determined to strike out for himself. His idea was, first, to rent land, furnish his own stock and farm implements, then after having paid for his stock, to buy land. I remember that when he announced this plan to us children we were so happy at the prospects of owning a wagon and a pair of mules and having only our father for boss that we shouted and leaped for joy.

Sure enough, he carried out his plans—in part, at least. He rented a farm of forty acres, for which he paid annually three bales of cotton, worth one hundred and fifty dollars. He bought a mule, a horse, and a yoke oxen, and so we started out for ourselves. The effort brought about a transformation in the spirits of the whole family. We all became better workers and for the first time began to take an interest in our work. However, before the crops were laid by, many troubles arose: one of our oxen broke his neck, one mule was attacked with some peculiar disease (I think they called it the "hooks"), and the horse became so poor and thin that he could not plow.

I shall never forget that mule. His ailment was a peculiar one; he could plow all day with ease, seemingly in perfect health, but after he lay down for the night he could not get up again. If we would help him to his feet, he would eat a good meal and work faithfully all day long. Consequently, the first thing I heard in the morning was my father's voice arousing me from sleep, saying, "Son, son, get up, day is breaking; let's go and lift the old mule up." We also had to call in a neighbor each morning. Toward the end of the season old Jim began to get so weak that it was difficult for him to do any plowing, and before the crop was laid by he gave out entirely.

At this juncture, not to be outdone, my brother and I took the mule's place at the plow, with my sister at the plow-handles, and in this way we helped to finish the crop after a fashion, so as to be ready to enter school the first day it opened in August.

The faithful ox that was left to us was always on hand, and it was my duty to plow and haul with him. In order to plow with an ox one has to put a half inch rope around his head, and let it extend to the plow-handles, for use as a line and bridle. That ox's head was so hard that a sore was cut into my hand, from jerking him for four years, and the scar is still there.

My father was without experience in self-direction and management, having always, up to that time, had a white man to direct him. As a consequence, our efforts to do business for ourselves was not wholly successful. I have already spoken of our trials during that first year. Things went well during the early part of the second year, and the crop was laid by with little mishap, except that my father, who plowed without shoes, stepped on the stub of a cane, which entering his foot, made him useless as a field-hand for the greater part of the year. I recall that father carried a piece of cane two inches long in his foot for more than a month, until he finally drew it to the surface by the application of fat meat poultices. How much better it would have been if he could have had a modern surgeon who would have drawn the splinter in two minutes. The crops were laid by, however, by the first of August, and we entered the school, where we remained for one month. Our corn crop that year was splendid. We gathered it and piled it in heaps in the field one Friday and Saturday. On Sunday there was a cloudburst, and all the corn was washed away by the little creek that passed through the plantation. This was a severe blow to us, one from which we were never wholly able to recover.

However, we struggled on. The next year, just as we

were ready to gather our crop, a disease called the "slow fever" broke out in our family. It was a great scourge and all the more serious because we were not able to employ a physician and because my father was compelled to be away from home during the day, working for food to keep us alive. My brother Lewis was born in the midst of this raging epidemic, and my mother was not able to leave her bed to wait on those who were sick. The only attention we got was that which neighbors could give, during the little time that they could spare from picking their own cotton. Although I never took to my bed during the two months that we suffered, I was almost as sick as any of the family. Mother had us put in little beds that hovered round her bed, and she waited on us the best she could until she was almost exhausted. But, in spite of her efforts, Lola, my oldest sister, and the most beloved member of the family, died. I distinctly remember that this so affected me that I did not care to live any longer. The fact is, I wanted to join her, for in my youthful mind I felt that she was better off than we were. It was after she had been buried and after we had returned from the little cemetery, all of us being still far from well, that I heard my father pray his first prayer before the family altar. The calamity was a great blow to him and brought about a change in his life that lasted as long as he lived.

The fourth and last year that we tried to get on by our initiative we had several unique experiences. At the end of that year, we came out so far in debt that, after we had paid our creditors all the cotton we had made, they came and took our corn, and, finally, the vegetables from our little garden as well as the pig. I felt that we ought to fight and not to allow all our substance to be taken from us, and I told my father so, but he insisted that we must obey the law. My mother, however, was a woman with considerable fire in her make-up. When they came and entered the crib to take the corn we children commenced to cry; then my mother came out and with considerable warmth demanded that a certain amount of corn be left there. She said that was the law. I do not know how she knew anything about the law, but I do know that the white man who was getting the corn respected her knowledge of the law and left there the amount of corn that she demanded. Having succeeded thus far, she demanded that he leave the chickens and vegetables alone, and this he also did. However, we were so completely broken up at this time that we applied to a white man for a home on his place—a home under the old system. My father only lived a short while after that, and he was never able again to lift himself from the condition of a share tenant.

On the morning of Christmas Day, 1889, my father seated himself on the roots of a large oak tree in the yard just after breakfast, and, calling me to him, said: "Son, you are nearing manhood, and you have no education. Besides, if you remain with me till you are twenty-one, I will not be able to help you. For these reasons, your mother and I have decided to set you free, provided you will make us one promise—that you will educate yourself."

By that time Mother had come up, and there we all stood. My mother and I were crying, and I am not sure that my father was not. I accepted the proposition and hurried off across the forest, where about a mile away I secured work with a white man, at thirty cents a day and board. Although we usually took a week for Christmas, that day my Christmas ended. I was very much excited. It was difficult for me to restrain myself. I was free. I was now to enjoy that longed-for opportunity of being my own master. The white man for whom I worked could neither read nor write. For that reason I feared to let him see me with books lest he should resent it, but nothing ever came of my apprehensions.

At the end of six months, I ran across quite accidentally —I will say providentially—the *Tuskegee Student,* a little paper published by the Tuskegee Normal and Industrial Institute, at Tuskegee, Alabama. In it there was the following note:

"There is an opportunity for a few able-bodied young men to make their way through school, provided they are willing to work. Applications should be made to Booker T. Washington, Principal."

I scribbled up some sort of application and addressed it simply to "Booker T. Washington," with nothing else on the envelope. All the same, it reached him, and I was admitted. . . .

5

FROM

In Spite of the Handicap

by James D. Corrothers

(1869–1917)

*In the 1840's fugitive slaves were making their way to-
ward an area of Michigan known as "the Chain Lake
Region." They settled there, set up their own government
and prospered. Free Negroes and the former slaves of
conscience-stricken owners swelled their ranks, and by
the 1860's the region had developed into a unique Negro
community.*

*James Corrothers was born into this settlement on July
2, 1869. When he was only two his family moved north
to South Haven, a predominantly white community, where
he was brought up by his grandfather who was Scotch,
Irish and Indian.*

*Corrothers was educated at Northwestern University,
and went from bootblack to minister and poet, but he
admits in his autobiography, "I have often regretted my
lack of early contact with the masses of my race. I have
. . . to learn their moods and methods . . . as an observer."*

*We tend to think of the race riot as a distinctly twen-
tieth-century event, associated with the explosive tensions*

145

of a long, hot, city summer. This next piece, unfortunately, dispels such a notion, for it recounts one such grim episode in the life of a small, Midwestern town during the late 1870's.

SOUTH HAVEN was, in those days, a tiny lumber town and lake port in Michigan, about eighty miles north-east from Chicago, across the lake. It was also a fruit-growing center, being located in the famous "Michigan Fruit Belt." In those days, that part of Michigan was pretty rough, as all newly settled communities are. People loved fisticuffs. Being the only coloured boy in the village, I had to thrash nearly every white boy in town before I was allowed to go to school in peace. Often, during my first months in school, I was soundly flogged by the teachers and deprived of my recesses, sometimes, I felt, quite unjustly. But this did not affect my determination to go to school. Such whippings as the teachers administered to me—properly or otherwise—I took, and came back the next day with my books. I was soon leading most of my classes, and the teachers were plainly interested in helping me forward. The boys, too, soon accepted me as a play-fellow. I had harboured no resentment against them or the teachers. I was simply *"new"* among them and they had to get used to me. Some of the teachers, like the children, had, perhaps, never seen a coloured boy before.

Grandfather and I lived alone together. We were very poor. Such luxuries as white sugar, coffee and tea we never had, but substituted for these "sassafras root," which we dug from the ground; and brown sugar. We mended our own shoes, and sometimes burned "driftwood" which we picked up from the lake beach. I never possessed an overcoat nor wore underwear until I began to support myself. I never had a new suit of clothing nor a single toy in all my boyhood; and I never wore "knee pants" in my life. My clothing consisted of Grandfather's old garments, turned wrong-side-out and cut down by him to as near my size as he could guess. In the fall and winter, as the weather grew colder, I put on additional clothing until, sometimes, I was wearing three and four suits at once. This was a common practice even among the white boys out there in those times. But I was, without doubt, the most bepatched boy in the town. Nevertheless, I was healthy and happy, and as well, if not better, read than most boys of my age in the village.

Grandfather was devoutly religious. Never a morning or evening but we had prayers, read scripture and sang a hymn. He could not legibly write his own name, nor correctly spell it; and his reading was crude and laborious: "A-n-d, and; t-h-e, the; L-o-r-d, Lord." *That* was the way of it. But with what meaning and earnestness. He was a man much beloved by both white and coloured people of the community for his kindness of heart, industry and honesty. I do not think he had an enemy in the village. The children, especially, loved him. He had no Negro blood whatever, being Scotch-Irish and Indian, but, having married a coloured woman, my grandmother, he was identified with the race. Through his father, he was descended from "The House of Carruthers" (I "made up" *my* spelling of the name when a boy) of Dumfries, Scotland. His mother was a Cherokee Indian woman. He had been a great hunter and traveller. The boys of the village loved to hear his tales. He had visited South America, Cuba, Haiti, Mexico and Canada; and had been in nearly all our states and territories, and had fought Indians. He had been married four times, and had outlived all his wives. My grandmother, his second wife, was a black woman of the Zulu race. My mother had considerable French blood from her mother, but her father was a black man whose ancestors were from Madagascar. Madecassee blood is easily distinguishable among coloured people by certain characteristics, such as nearly Caucasian features and almost straight, black hair. My maternal grandfather, I am told, was in unusual demand as a country fiddler.

There were only two coloured people in our town, when I was a boy, who could read a newspaper. Of these I happened to be one. The other was a young man named "Jim" Green whom the Union soldiers brought back from the South, a little boy, at the close of the war. The best white families in town had "brought him up," and he clerked in a large drygoods store. He was quite an aristocrat. I always felt thankful if he even spoke to me.

Sometimes, on Sunday afternoons, Green would read the *Chicago Times* or the *Inter Ocean* to a group of coloured people about him. At other times this proud duty devolved upon me. I distinctly remember how, when the news did not appear to satisfy my hearers, I would add an occasional phrase or sentence to suit their ideas, or set them laughing. Nobody dreamed that, a few years afterward, I would be "doing space" (reporting) on those very papers.

There were some very remarkable Negro characters in Michigan in my early boyhood. They were the product and antidote of the peculiar conditions of those times. The Negroes had but recently been emancipated, and the North was not used to them. In several small towns in Michigan and Indiana they were not allowed to live; in some they might not even remain over night, purchase food, nor obtain a drink of water. The unfortunate Negro who unwittingly entered such a community was first made to sing and dance then given a few kicks and cuffs and told to "trot." And forthwith he "trotted." No second intimation was ever necessary.

One of the strange characters whose physical prowess did much to change these conditions was Dave Adly, a sort of larger black Fitzsimmons who called himself "The Black Tiger." He was not like other men, but seemed a sort of physical "leftover" from the days of primal man. He had a strength not common to men, and loved nothing so much as an opportunity to prove it. He was double-jointed, long-armed, and gorilla-chested; and, when angry, roared like an animal. The fame of this unusual man spread all over lower Michigan, Indiana and portions of Ohio; and, in spots, along the upper Mississippi. Whenever Adly heard of a town where coloured men had been made to dance and run, he went there and gave them a chance to try the same thing on him. The usual result was that the next Negro who happened along was let strictly alone. When aroused, Adly was a battle-glaring demon upon whom showers of stones and clubs seemed to have no other effect than to increase his inhuman rage. A man who foolishly drew a pistol, once, to shoot him had his arm snapped in a twinkling, and for hours afterward lay stunned and bleeding from the effect of a terrible blow from Adly's open hand. For, in his mêlées, Adly seemed omniscient and invincible, and always emerged from them triumphant and vainglorious.

There was a *reason* for such Negroes as he: Certain slave owners had bred Negroes carefully and skilfully, like blooded draft-horses, to produce super-humanly powerful working machines. Adly was a "working machine" gone wrong. I have personally seen Adly who is, of course, long since dead. He was quite an old man when I was a boy.

There were several other Negroes, somewhat of the Adly type, though less powerful—such men as "Blood" Tyler and the seven Howard brothers, cousins of Tyler —who were well known for their exploits in lower Michigan and Indiana during my early boyhood; but they and the well-nigh unthinkable conditions under which coloured people were sometimes made to suffer in the North and Middle West have passed away, and there is no need to relate mere details concerning them. My purpose has been honestly to set down something of the actual conditions into which I was born, "in the free North," a little more than forty years ago.* *The North was not used to coloured people.*

I recall an amusing experience of my boyhood which may serve to illustrate this statement: Once, in passing a white farmer's house a few miles out of South Haven, the farmer accosted me with: "Say, little boy, just you wait in the road there a minute. My little boy never saw a *coloured* boy, and I don't want him to miss this chance."

I waited, obligingly.

Soon a little boy of about eight years came out of the house, his eyes fairly popping with astonishment.

"What makes your face so dirty, little boy?" he asked, curiously.

"I'm not *dirty;* I'm *coloured,*" I informed him. "*God* made me this colour," I said.

"Well, can't you wash it off?"

"No," I explained, "I'll always *be* this way."

His last shot was: *"How can you tell when your face is dirty?"*

The first mobbing of Negroes of which I ever heard did not occur in the South, but in Michigan; and in the town where I was raised. It happened in this way:

A great Fourth of July celebration was being given in our little town, and a number of excursions poured into it, by boat and train, from Chicago, Kalamazoo and other points, swelling the population of the little town from its normal size of 1200 to perhaps 10,000 or more, for the day. But to the credit of South Haven let it be said that the trouble was started by sailors and visiting strangers, and not by the citizens of the town.

It was a mere trifle that started the trouble: A bit of fisticuffs between a coloured boy from Kalamazoo and a white boy from the country. This grew into a general

_____
* 1869

fracas between the friends of the two boys, and developed into a race riot in which Negroes were beaten and chased, like rabbits. Soon the triumphant whites were running, like madmen, through the streets yelling:

"Fifty cents for a nigger! A dollar for a nigger! Five dollars for a nigger! Just one more *nigger!*"

Negroes hid in the woods; in graveyards, and under sidewalks, or ran past the depot toward which, in panic fear, their flight had been directed. Some burrowed into the ground, and hid there for days. One Negro barber who was quite a linguist and a dandy, was knocked, swearing, down a flight of stairs; another Negro was chased into the river; another, a comical old fellow by the name of Reuben Berry, was found eating a pie in a restaurant, and was pretty badly smashed and kicked about. "Reuben didn't want no mo' pie!" he declared afterward. That no one was killed in this riot seems almost miraculous. But a number of coloured people were severely beaten and scarred for life. I was personally not molested, though I was in the streets at the time. None of my relatives were hurt by the rioters whose anger appeared to be principally directed against the members of the gaudily uniformed coloured band from Kalamazoo, several of whom at first defied the whites, but later, fled for their lives.

The little town has always been ashamed of this black spot on its history, and has tried, in every way possible, to make the "*amende honourable*" to its coloured citizens. A year or so after its unfortunate "Mob Fourth" its white citizens gave an elaborate "Emancipation Celebration" at which all coloured people were their guests. Frederick Douglass was invited to be the orator of the day, but did not come. A year later, however, he spoke in a grove for the coloured people of Covert, nine miles from South Haven. My father was Grand Marshal of the Day upon that occasion. Douglass was then the recognised race leader, as was the late Booker T. Washington.

Times grew very hard in South Haven; and Grandfather was getting old. So, when I was about fourteen years old, we decided to make our home with an uncle of mine by the name of Henry, Grandfather's eldest son, in Muskegon, Michigan, a busy lumber city, where I could get work in the mills. We settled such debts as we had; bade our neighbors farewell, and placed our few belongings on board a small, two-masted schooner, upon which we also took passage. Soon the wind rose; the white seamen hoisted sail, and we were gone. We took our last look together at the little town, nestling in its woody cove at the mouth of "Black river"; we scanned its deep gullies; its picturesque, wooden bridges; the grove; the little, droning sawmill; the stores; the quiet shady streets and the white, sandy beach, until all at last became a distant blur across the widening expanse of Lake Michigan.

III

THE TWENTIETH CENTURY:

The Bitter Legacy

THE CIVIL WAR destroyed the economic basis of the South, and, as a result, both white and Negro groped for a way to earn a livelihood from the land. As previously described by William Holtzclaw, a system was developed whereby a Negro family was assigned to work a particular piece of property owned by a planter, and the family would receive a share of the crops for wages. Since the tenants were furnished by the planter with supplies on which to live during the year, and for which they mortgaged their share of the crops to come, the planter used this opportunity to charge exorbitant rates for these supplies. At the end of the farming season the tenants were lucky not to be in debt to the planter.

In the first two decades of the twentieth century two things happened to encourage the Negro to leave the land in the South and try his luck in the cities to the North and West. The first event was a disastrous boll weevil attack which by 1921 had ruined cotton crops throughout the South and made the landlords turn, in great number, to livestock and dairying. The second incentive was World War I, which took a large percentage of white workers out of industry and into military service. Many Negroes in the South saw this as their opportunity to get jobs in the North. The great migration began.

Since 1910 the Negro population has increased fivefold outside the Deep South. Fifty years ago about three-fourths of the Negro population lived in rural areas. Today it is just the opposite. Three out of four Negro families live in the city. But it has been a frightfully disillusioning experience. Housing discrimination resulted in crowded ghetto tenements. Unemployment was high and the jobs that were available offered low pay. Poverty became the norm. Educational facilities were poor and a serious dropout problem was created. The family unit was unstable, a carry-over from slavery days when Negro families often did not live together and the father was often unknown. In 1960 one in eleven white families was headed by a female; one in five nonwhite families had a female head.

Children were hurt most by these conditions. Sibling rivalry mounted with material scarcity. Youngsters were farmed out to relatives because of broken homes. Their self-esteem was low and they found little desire to identify with their family. They took to the streets.

A vicious circle was created. Robert G. Goodwin, in *America Is for Everybody,* pointed out that job discrimination and lack of educational opportunity limit employment opportunities and result in low and unstable incomes. He wrote, "Low incomes, combined with discrimination, reduce attainable levels of health and skills, and thus limit occupational choice and income in the future. And limited job opportunities result in limited availability of education and apprenticeship training, thus completing the circle." *

This is the bitter legacy.

---

* Robert G. Goodwin, *America Is for Everybody* (U.S. Dept. of Labor, Government Printing Office, 1963).

1

FROM

His Eye Is on the Sparrow

by Ethel Waters with Charles Samuels

(1900–   )

Growing up in the slums of Philadelphia at the turn of the century meant growing up fast. It meant learning to accept prostitution, opium-smoking, heroin addiction, and various forms of depravity as a way of life. It meant learning all about sex at the age of three, tending a syphilis-ridden whore at the age of ten, and becoming a family provider at the age of twelve by mastering the art of shoplifting. It is the kind of growing up that forces us to reevaluate our notions of childhood, for it is remarkable that Ethel Waters survived at all. Her rise to fame and fortune as an actress and blues singer is a tribute to the resiliency of childhood, and her own faith in God and herself. And yet we must wonder: for every Ethel Waters, how many children, and how many of their children's children, are living out their lives today in such conditions, with not even the faintest hope of escape?

I DID have one childhood home for more than a few weeks. It was a three-room shanty in an alley just off Clifton Street. Prostitution was legal in Philadelphia then, and

Clifton Street, located in the old Bloody Eighth Ward, lay in the heart of the red-light district.

There was always something interesting to watch in that lively neighborhood. Every night the whores, black and white, paraded up and down Clifton Street. They all wore the same outfit, a regular uniform consisting of a voile skirt with taffeta underneath, cork-heeled shoes, a black velvet neckband, and big whores' hoop earrings. Of course their unmistakable trademark was their hip-wriggling walk.

I was not yet six years old when we moved there and seven when we left, but I had one hell of a time for myself in that plague spot of vice and crime. I came to know well the street whores, the ladies in the sporting houses, their pimps, the pickpockets, shoplifters, and other thieves who lived all around us. I played with the thieves' children and the sporting women's trick babies. It was they who taught me how to steal.

Things at home didn't change much, but I remember that little alley home as the heaven on earth of my childhood. For once we were all together in a whole house—Vi, Ching, Charlie, me, Mom on her days off. And after a while Louise also came to live with us.*

We stayed in Clifton Street for fifteen months. That was the only time I could feel that I had a family that wasn't continually disrupting and belonged in one neighborhood. My family kept on squabbling, but I lived more in the street than at home.

All of us dead-end kids ran errands for the whores. Some of them were good for as much as fifteen, twenty, or twenty-five cents in tips. We spent most of our earnings on candy and food. You could buy a frankfurter for three cents at a street stand, yat-gaw-mein cost a nickel in the Chinese joints, and for a dime you could get a whole plate

---

* Vi and Ching were Ethel's aunts; Charlie an uncle. Mom was her grandmother and Louise her mother.

of fish and French-fried potatoes at a food stand called See Willie's.

A bunch of us would often sleep all night out on the street, over the warm iron gratings of bakeries or laundries. Our families didn't care where we were, and these nesting places, when you put your coat under you, were no more uncomfortable than the broken-down beds with treacherous springs or the bedbug-infested pallets we had at home. Being so large for my age, I was accepted as an equal by older boys and girls. My biggest asset as a street child in the tenderloin was my ability to keep my mouth shut.

Along with a few other Clifton Street youngsters I acted as a semi-official lookout girl for the sporting houses. Though prostitution was a legalized business, there were occasional police raids. These came when the church groups bore down heavily on the authorities or after one body too many, stabbed, shot, or cut up very untidily, had been found in some dark alley.

Any of us slum children could smell out a cop even though he was a John, a plain-clothes man. These brilliant sleuths never suspicioned that we were tipsters for the whole whoring industry. Usually we'd be playing some singing game on the street when we spotted a cop, a game like Here Comes Two Dudes A-Riding or the one that begins:

> *King William was King James's son,*
> *Upon his breast he wore a star,*
> *And that was called . . .*

On smelling out the common enemy, we boys and girls in the know would start to shout the songs, accenting certain phrases. If we happened to be playing a singing game we'd whistle the agreed-on tune. The other kids, even those who weren't lookouts, would innocently imitate us, and in no time at all the whole neighborhood would be alerted. The street women would disappear, the lights would go out, and the doors would be locked in the sporting houses.

Some of the friendlier policemen tried to be nice to us, but that got them nowhere. It was an unwritten law among us not to accept candy from cops or have anything to do with them. It was the only law that was never broken on Clifton Street.

The Bloody Eighth at that time was not exclusively a Negro slum. We had plenty of white neighbors, Hunkies and Jews, and some Chinese. The few respectable families, white and black, forced by circumstances to live in that slum kept to themselves as much as possible.

I didn't know much about color then. There was no racial prejudice at all in that big melting pot running over with vice and crime, violence, poverty, and corruption. I never was made to feel like an outcast on Clifton Street. All of us, whites and blacks, and yellows, were outcasts there together and having a fine time among ourselves.

Anyway, racial prejudice couldn't have existed in that neighborhood where vice was the most important business. The white and Negro street whores worked together, lived and slept together. The two men who owned and protected most of them were Lovey Joe and Rosebud, both of them Negroes. It was not considered unusual for a colored prostitute to have a trick baby white as a lily.

I've always had great respect for whores. The many I've known were kind and generous. Some of them supported whole families and kept at their trade for years to send their trick babies through college. I never knew a prostitute who did harm to anyone but herself. I except, of course, the whores who are real criminals and use knockout drops and bring men to their rooms to be robbed, beaten, and blackmailed.

No woman in my immediate family ever turned to prostitution. Neither were they saints. Sometimes they lived with men they weren't married to. This was true of my mother and my two aunts, Vi and Ching. And they never saw anything wrong in getting what presents they could from their men—shoes for themselves or for me, clothes, or money.

My grandmother hated the idea of my growing up in the red-light district and strongly disapproved of prostitution. But there was nothing she could do about it. The alley shanty was the best home she could find or afford.

And Mom had no objection at all to doing the weekly laundry of the prostitutes. However, they had to address her respectfully as Mrs. Perry or she wouldn't take their work. Mom used that name all of the years she was in love with Pop Sam Perry, who was a huckster and had his own little vegetable wagon. Vi and Ching also insisted that their prostitute customers treat them with dignity and respect.

We had one family link, though, with prostitution. This was Blanche, one of Mom's nieces, who was only seven or eight years older than I. Though Mom shook her head over Blanche's way of life, she was always strongly biased in her favor because she was our relative.

Being hardly more than a child herself, Blanche often played with me, read me stories, and sang little songs with me. Her beauty fascinated me. I loved her. There was a great camaraderie between us, and that young prostitute gave me some of the attention and warm affection I was starving for. Whenever I tipped off the sporting world that the cops were just around the corner I felt I was doing it for Blanche and her friends.

Mom herself always did Blanche's laundry, and I delivered it each week. In her room I saw the equipment used by a woman in her profession. I never commented or asked questions about it but used my eyes and ears. I never was a child to pretend ignorance to learn more about something that aroused my curiosity.

Blanche soon decided that she could trust me completely. Lovey Joe, the pimp, a huge, kindly man, was her sweetheart, and she'd send messages to him through me. Whenever they quarreled Lovey Joe would find me on the street and give me notes to deliver to Blanche. Afterward he was always able to sweet-talk himself into her affections.

Later Blanche got into the habit of sending me to the druggist with a sealed envelope. He'd give me bi-chloride of mercury, blue ointment, and larkspur. Blanche had syphilis which we called the Pox. She had a horrible sore on her upper leg that eventually became so painful she couldn't bear to bathe it herself. So I would wash it for her, apply the medicines, and help her pull on the specially made stocking she had to wear.

Blanche was in and out of my life until I was twelve. In the last stages of her life, and still not twenty years old, she took to sniffing coke and using the bang needles to forget the pain. From that same drugstore I got the dope she had to have.

I have never forgotten that sweet, lovely-looking and enchanting Blanche and what it was like to watch her decay and rot before my eyes. I'd see her at night, all dressed up and gay, and then the next day so ripped and pounded by pain.

The prettiest sight in the whole neighborhood came at dusk when the lights were turned on in the sporting houses. I'd stand on the street and look in with awe at the rich, highly polished furniture and the beautiful women sitting at the windows wearing low-cut evening gowns or kimonos. Some of them put on aprons.

But there was Blanche—and others. Prostitution and dope never could afterward tempt me. Blanche, poor soul, did more to keep me straight in the tough years to come than any person I ever knew. I also never have touched liquor except for medicinal purposes because I saw as a child what whisky and gin can do to people. I don't smoke because cigarettes are forever associated in my mind with the drinking and chaos there. I don't gamble because I know what trouble *that* can bring.

Whatever moral qualities I have, come, I'm afraid, from all the sordidness and evil I observed firsthand as a child. However, I do not wish to exaggerate the impact on me of the evil that constantly surrounded me when I was little. I was tough always and, like all slum kids, was able quickly to adjust myself to any and all situations.

God's hand must have closed over me very early in life, making me tough and headstrong and resilient. It is His hand that has carried me safely down the long, dark road I've had to follow since.

In crowded slum homes one's sex education begins very early indeed. Mine began when I was about three and sleeping in the same room, often in the same bed, with my aunts and my transient "uncles." I wasn't fully aware of what was going on but resented it. By the time I was seven I was repelled by every aspect of sex.

Being so enormous for my age, I didn't escape the attentions of the fully grown men in the neighborhood who liked little girls. The first thing that I discovered about sporting men, society's despised pimps, was that they had a much more moral attitude toward kids than many of the squares around Clifton Street.

Lovey Joe, Rosebud, and the others had a strict "Hands off!" code with little girls. I think they would have beaten to death any other pimp who molested one of us youngsters.

Actually, being such a wise-up child, I don't think I was ever in too much danger from degenerates. Nobody was handing me any package. My vile tongue was my shield, my toughness my armor. With my gutter vocabulary and my aggressiveness I outshocked the odd ones. When I wanted to tell anyone off I began with the four-letter words.

I like to think I am remembered with a horrified head-to-toe shudder by at least one fully grown man who lived in the old Bloody Eighth Ward.

When he made a grab for me I closed my fist and slammed it down hard on the anatomical feature he most treasured. I put him out of amorous action, I imagine, for weeks.

Through my mother, this temporarily disabled child lover complained to Mom that I had slugged him under the belt when he tried to pat me in a paternal manner.

After questioning me Sally accepted my interpretation of the incident and sent this message to the wounded gent: "I'll cut your throat if you ever come near Ethel again."

When Louise joined us in Clifton Street it was because she'd been having a little woman trouble. Pop Norman chased the women—and vice versa. One of Pop Norman's bright flames became so bold and giddy with infatuation that she came to Louise's house to flaunt her intimacy with my stepfather.

I've mentioned that Louise, like my aunts, Mom, and me, had an insanely violent temper. No matter what she had done, she afterward knew neither remorse or pity.

My mother and the bright flame tangled. During the fight Louise picked up a railroad spike and beat the other woman so badly with it that she had to be taken to the hospital. Louise left Genevieve, my stepsister, with Norman's parents and came to live with us. She stayed until the Chester police lost interest in the case.

I'd always been told that Louise was my mother. That hadn't meant anything to me because I always called my grandmother Mom and felt so much closer to her. But when Louise moved into the shanty I began to realize she was my mother and came to like her. But she never liked me. She merely tolerated me.

Yet once, while in Clifton Street, I did feel she cared for me with a mother's affection. When I was six I suffered an attack of typhoid fever and double pneumonia and was taken to the Pennsylvania Hospital, where Louise was working as an attendant. When the doctors there told Louise I might die, some of the long-repressed maternal love seemed to come to life in her. She spent as much time as she could at my bedside. Every time I opened my eyes Louise seemed to be there, looking down at me with tenderness and apprehension.

Sally Anderson had always inclined to the Catholic faith. When she learned that I might survive my illness Mom sent for Father Healey of St. Peter Claver R.C. Church. He baptised and anointed me.

After I recovered, Louise went back into her shell, ignoring me as much as possible. She always lavished all her mother's love on Genevieve. If she couldn't love me, I suppose it was because I was the living reminder of the most frightening day of her life.

We had no Sunday things on Clifton Street. The stores and other businesses were open as on every other day. The nearest we came to religious observance of the Sabbath was listening to street preachers. And none of us dead-end kids knew what it was like to go off with the family on a Sunday picnic or to the bathing beaches.

Pop Sam Perry was always kind to me and would take me for a walk sometimes on Sunday. "Dress Ethel up," he'd say, "I want to take her out." Hand in hand, we'd walk through the bleak, dreary streets, looking into the shopwindows and ending up with a visit in an ice cream parlor.

Whenever Pop Sam Perry had an argument with Mom I knew enough to keep away from her. When things weren't going well in Mom's love life she seemed to take it out on me.

But at all other times I was her favorite. For me there was one pleasant feature about her militant weekly home-comings. Mom always came home with "cold functions" for me.

In those days most of the white people who had Negro servants preferred to throw leftover food in the garbage pail rather than give it to the people who worked so hard for them around the house.

Early in life Mom figured out a way to outwit her white bosses. She sewed little pockets in an apron and filled the pockets with neatly done up parcels of food—sand-wiches, pieces of pie or cake, sugar, and eggs. Then when she was ready to take her day off on Thursday she'd put on the heavily laden apron under her petticoat. Mom could sneak any kind of food out of her boss's house ex-cept soup.

The parcels were my "cold functions." When I was very little I'd pull up her dress and dive under it, yelling, "What did you bring me this time, Mom? What did you bring me?" Mom always got a big thrill out of that.

Sometimes, on days when she wasn't coming home, she worried about me not getting enough to eat. Whenever she could she'd fix up a parcel of food for me and leave it on a post or the garbage pail of the house where she was working, and I'd come out and get it.

But I can never remember Mom kissing or hugging me. She wasn't demonstrative, and I think she feared that Vi and Ching would resent her showing affection and make my life a living hell while she was out working. Vi, more than Ching, was always jealous of the way Mom tried to take care of me.

Being a tough-minded and realistic child, I can't say that Mom's home-comings gave me any great pleasure, despite the delicious "cold functions."

Only on the rare occasions when she found my aunts sober was there peace in the house. But almost always she'd come home and find them high—nasty and horrible on gin that cost ten cents a pint. Mom would bitch, chase their men friends out, then resume bitching and sometimes hit my aunts.

Fortunately, neither Vi nor Ching dared fight back. They seemed to realize, even when they were drunk, that Mom's terrible temper would drive her on and on until she killed or crippled them.

Once, though, Ching, the easier-going-one, did try hitting back. In her towering rage Mom bit a whole piece of flesh out of Ching's arm. Police questioned Ching when she was taken to the hospital, but she refused to tell who had bitten her. The next day I found my aunt's chunk of severed flesh on the floor.

Mom had the curious idea that she could keep me out of mischief by continually sending me on errands or by telling me to take a walk in the park. Hating the neighborhood as violently as she did, she always pulled the shades down low and wouldn't look out on the alley even if she heard an explosion out there. This permitted me to play in peace with children she disapproved of, right in front of my own door.

It was natural for children of the shoplifters and pickpockets to follow in their parents' footsteps. But, oddly enough, I never knew of a trick baby of a whore turning to prostitution. They learned from their own mother, as I had from my cousin Blanche, how big the pay-off is in suffering and misery.

These kids were older than me. They accepted me as an equal, not only because I was hep and so big for my age, but because they were awed by my atomic delivery of the King's profanity. Some of these words they had never heard before. Generally, with the children who were my friends, I shared my encyclopedic knowledge of bad words, offering precise definitions of what each term meant. I also saw fit to punish my enemies by refusing them this valuable information. Sometimes we initiates would stand on the street screaming curses at the top of our voices.

The older boys and girls who were my friends sometimes went into the darker alleys at night to make fumbling sex experiments. I was always happy to be their lookout, though I took no such pride in this as I did in singing and whistling warnings to the neighborhood brothels and street women. I myself made no such experiments. The other kids did largely out of curiosity. Usually, once their curiosity was satisfied, they quit experimenting, finding it more fun to steal and play street games. Sex didn't interest me. There was nothing about it I didn't know.

I got my kindergarten course in thievery when the pickpockets' kids showed me how to swipe bags of rolls and bottles of milk from doorsteps and porches. I displayed such adeptness that I soon was helping them raid stores of food. Before long I became their leader. In the end we stole so much that we exhausted the looting possibilities of the whole neighborhood and had to fan out into other sections for action.

I stole because I was always hungry. I'm still always hungry, now that I come to think of it. Whenever I remember the old days on Clifton Street I develop a lumberjack appetite. And I think of those days often. We never felt there was anything wrong in stealing. We never thought anything about it at all. We were hungry. I still don't know what's wrong about a kid stealing when he's hungry.

When my grandmother wasn't home I seldom sat down to a fully prepared meal. My aunts lived on liquor and seldom felt like eating much.

But after they found out that I was the best child thief

in the Bloody Eighth Ward my aunts occasionally decided that a cooked meal wouldn't kill them.

Whenever this happened they'd send me out with a quarter. If there was no cash in the house they'd have me gather up all the empty whisky and beer bottles in the shanty and return them. If there were not enough empties to get twenty-five cents for I'd be sent to the pawnshop to borrow a quarter on a new pair of shoes some admirer had given Vi or Ching.

Once I had the quarter, I was ready to go shopping and stealing. First I'd buy wood for three cents and charcoal for a nickel. Walking into the bakery, I'd order a loaf of yesterday's bread, which also cost three cents. When the man turned to get the bread from the shelf I'd slip a half dozen cinnamon buns into my big shopping bag.

In the butcher shop I'd ask for three cents' worth of cat or dog meat. The butchers on Clifton Street only had to look at my big hungry eyes to know that I didn't want the meat for any pet animal. They'd give me plenty of good scraps fit for human consumption.

Swiping plenty of fresh vegetables was the easiest job of all. If the owner was inside the store I'd just take my choice of the potatoes, onions, carrots, and peas lying on the stands outside his shop. If he was outside I'd order three cents' worth of salt or something else I knew he kept in the rear of his store. By the time he'd come out with it I'd have my bag full of vegetables covered up by the package of meat.

My ability to go out with a quarter and come back with a whole dinner—and some change—delighted my aunts. They never tired of praising my prowess.

I was a very good child thief.

I was never caught.

I only stopped stealing some years later while I was living in Chester. One day I went out, carrying a parasol, to the five-and-dime store. Because of its wide variety of merchandise this was the kind of store I most enjoyed robbing.

Everything I took—hair ribbons, Hershey bars, toys, and trinkets of all sorts—I dropped into my parasol. But when I came out of the store it was raining like mad. I couldn't open the parasol because all my loot would have fallen out.

I had to walk all the way home in the teeming rain, carrying the closed parasol. Everyone I met looked at it, then at me, as though I was crazy. Soaked to the skin, I indignantly decided petty larceny didn't pay if it made me get that wet.

Thereafter I only stole things once in a while to find out whether I still retained my magic touch. . . .

By the time I was eleven I was so big that I had trouble getting men to leave me alone. Several times Mom sent me to a doctor who examined me to find out if I was still a virgin. The doctor said I was but "might be going into a decline." This meant tuberculosis, so Mom gave me porter, beer, and ale to stimulate my appetite, milk being too dear for us to buy.

My grandmother also decided it was time I had some wholesome amusement. She took me to Pop Grey, an old friend of hers, who ran a respectable dance hall on South Street. Even though I was so much under the legal age he agreed to let me attend evening sessions at his place.

Admission cost fifty cents, but before long Pop offered to let me in free if I'd give his other girl customers dancing lessons. I won many prizes in dancing contests put on at Grey's. Besides the usual one-steps and waltzes, we did square dances and all the schottisches and quadrilles that have lately become so popular all over again.

I could always dance for hours without getting tired. The year before (I was ten but looked fifteen) I made Mabel, a girl friend of mine, take me to the Saturday-night dances at another hall in a dimly lighted place over a stable. Mabel was a little bit of a thing, but at fourteen she was as developed as she'd ever be.

To those Saturday-night dances I'd wear the high-heeled shoes I'd found at rummage sales. Though my hair reached to my waist, I'd put it up and pack it with rats, which were very fashionable just then.

I'd make my eyebrows bigger by using burnt cork. For cheek rouge I rubbed the red dye from crepe shelving paper into my face, topping it off with talcum powder. Proudly I hung whores' hoop earrings in my pierced ears and, for a last touch of class, tied a black velvet ribbon around my neck.

With my bucket-shaped head on a long, scrawny neck, topped by the mountain of built-up black hair, I'd hobble off to the dance on my rickety high-heeled shoes. I never doubted that I was the best-dressed girl there.

I kept believing that, even after I heard a woman friend tell Louise:

"I saw a freak at the dance last Saturday night. She looked just like your Ethel." It was me she'd seen, of course, but she couldn't believe her eyes.

Fortunately, my mother didn't catch on and I was able to keep going to those wonderful Saturday-night dances, feeling always like the belle of the ball and a dream girl in my outlandish getup.

The last little place Mom was able to set up for us was in an alley off Kater Street. This was in a semi-red-light district of Philadelphia. In some ways it was even tougher than Clifton Street. Whenever I entered the alley on my way home I walked to the shanty with my face turned to the wall. This was the only way I could avoid seeing the whores emptying the pockets of the sailors and other men who were making love to them right in the open.

The common toilet in the alley had to be locked inside and out. The outside lock kept out the hookers and their customers. The inside lock was for the protection of me and the other young girls who lived in the alley.

Kater Street was almost the end of the road for Mom. When she got home she was so tired and groaning with her many aches and pains. But her children—Vi, Charlie, Ching, and Louise—were still plaguing her.

I felt very sorry for Mom, but I didn't let that interrupt my mischief-making. Across a fence from our shanty was the back yard of a restaurant called the Busy Bee. Every chance I got I gathered up garbage and other refuse and threw it into the baskets of potatoes, lettuce, and other vegetables which lay exposed in the yard.

Going into the house, I'd wait patiently at the window for the restaurant men to come out of the kitchen to get the baskets. When they saw my garbage on their nice clean vegetables they'd cry out in anguish:

"What's this? What sons of bitches have been here? Dammit to hell, what stuff is this?"

Utterly charmed by my ability to throw them into a frenzy, I'd then go out and ask people I met on the street, "What restaurant do you eat in?"

If they replied, "The Busy Bee," I'd laugh with joy until I became hysterical. Puzzled, they'd always want to know what I was laughing at. But giving them only a pitying look, I'd walk on until I met someone else who said he patronized the Busy Bee. Then I would get hysterical all over again.

In Kater Street I learned another lesson you'll find in the book called *What Every Young Girl Should Know*, a lesson about opium and the sort of people who smoke it.

Back in Clifton Street I'd learned a little about the other narcotics—cocaine, morphine, and heroin. And I'd heard my aunts call Harry, a friend of my mother's and a sneak thief, a junkie. But I'd never known quite what that meant. When I thought of Harry, "the junkie," I remembered his high and flighty eyes.

While we were on Kater Street my aunts were again earning their drinking money by doing the sporting women's laundry. They sent me out to get and deliver the wash. Whenever I took the weekly bundle to a customer I called Miss Hazel I had to wait a long time after knocking on her door before it was opened. And her eyes, like Harry's, were high and flighty. Sometimes there was a curious smell—an odor like yeast—in the hall.

One day when Miss Hazel asked me to do some errands for her I said, "That funny smell ain't in the hallway today."

"What funny smell?"

I described it.

Miss Hazel nodded. "Ethel," she said, "any time you notice that in the hallway, let me know—ring my bell three times. That will be our signal. Okay?"

Unknowingly I'd saved her from a police raid. The yeasty smell was the odor of opium cooking. Miss Hazel hadn't known it was escaping from her rooms into the hallway.

After that she felt more free with me. She'd let me into her room, something she'd never done before. I didn't comment on what I saw there—wet towels and sheets spread across the windows and the door, silent, sleepy-looking people in the room, the little lamp sitting on the floor.

Before very long Miss Hazel trusted me to the point of asking me to stay with her when she smoked alone. She paid me a dollar just for stroking her temples while she smoked.

Sometimes her boy friend would come in, take off his coat, lie down, and smoke. Miss Hazel knew how to prepare and cook the stuff. The little black opium pellets looked like pine tar. She'd put her head in my lap as she lay down to smoke.

"These are my kicks," Miss Hazel would say.

I never forgot that dark room, the wet sheets hanging over the door, or that yeasty smell. I never forgot watching the torment of Miss Hazel and her friends when they couldn't get dope. My aunts were like that when they couldn't get liquor. They'd become frantic, would get the shakes, be thrown into utter chaos. And what they were going mad for was fifteen minutes of artificial stimulation.

Going around with girls of fourteen or fifteen when I was eleven, I was continually embarrassed because they had breasts and I was as flat as a board. I made many experiments with falsies, which I had seen prostitutes wearing. My luck was bad; half the time one falsie would be up around my shoulder and the other down on my hip.

The other girls never stopped talking about their sweethearts, so I invented a boy friend for myself. He was handsome, loaded with money, generous, and out of his mind about me. He was also strictly anonymous, and that was what I appreciated most about him. I had no boy friend and I wanted none. All I wanted was to talk about him.

These girls were of a better class than I'd known before, but hotly interested in sex. Often as I walked home from school with them one would suggest, "Let's stop in this place."

The place would be the home or the store of some middle-aged man who had a yen for young girls. The moment I saw him I'd dig him, dig the place, dig the situation. I'd watch, showing no surprise as the man fondled the young girls, played with their childlike breasts, and slapped them over the behind.

These older girls, knowing I was hep to sex, trusted me not to tell on them. But I must have had a chilling eye because none of the men ever touched me or even tried to.

Strong as a bull at eleven, I'd taken a job as cleaning woman for Giuseppe Donato, the sculptor. I got seventy-five cents a week for working after school for him. Besides cleaning up his studio, I kept his big stove full of egg coal. Mr. Donato predicted I'd have a pretty figure when I grew up.

With Mom so full of the misery, I thought a lot about her and all she'd tried to do for me. When fall came I decided to give her the only good Christmas she'd ever had.

By saving my money for months, I managed to amass five dollars. On Christmas Eve I bought a tiny tree, put it on the table, and decorated it. I also bought three fancy little glasses, the kind Mom liked, set them out in a row before the tree with a dollar bill stuck in each one. I didn't buy any food, knowing that Mom would come home with enough "cold functions" for dinner.

Ching was away, and there was only Vi at home. For weeks I'd begged her to be sober on this one Christmas Eve. "That will mean so much to Mom," I kept saying. "It will make her so happy."

But Vi wasn't there when Mom came in, tired and all beat up. When she saw the tree all decorated and the little glasses with the dollar bills in them her whole face lighted up.

"This is nice, Ethel," she said. "This makes me feel good."

She sat down at the table, and I sat down on the other side. The idea that some of the family had thought of her this Christmas gave her a wonderful, warm thrill. It was nice for me, too, feeling close to her, talking to her so peacefully. I kept looking across the tiny tree at her smiling face.

We sat there, and it was as though Mom at last had the home and the family she wanted.

We sat there like that, feeling happy and lighthearted, until we heard Vi outside and let her in. She was drunk and bullish.

"Why did you have to get drunk this one day, Vi?" I

asked her. "This one day I asked you to stay sober so Mom could have a nice Christmas."

Vi started calling me horrible names. I went over to the steps leading upstairs and sat down. I didn't answer her curses, just stared at her.

"Don't pay her no mind, Ethel," said Mom. "Leave her be. Let her get it all out of her system."

Vi fell into a chair and continued to upbraid and curse me. I said nothing, just kept watching her. Seeing something on the floor, Vi swayed down and picked it up. It was a hatchet. I didn't move, but never took my eyes off her.

"Put down that hatchet, Vi," said Mom. "Put it down. Have you lost your mind?"

Vi pulled back her arm and threw the hatchet at me with all her strength. I didn't have time to fall out of the way, just managed to move my head sideways as it flew across the room. It went into the wall in back of me with a quivering, zinging noise. It had gone over my shoulder, missing my head by inches.

I got up and jumped on Vi. I don't remember anything after that. I was temporarily insane and I must have choked and punched, kicked and gouged Vi in my maniacal fury. All I can remember after that was being pulled off Vi by Mom and a fat man who lived next door. He had rushed in on hearing Vi's screams. It was that fat man who pried my hands from Vi's throat and stopped me from killing her. I never would have let go by myself until she was dead.

Vi was unconscious, out. They gave her ammonia and smelling salts, then they carried her upstairs and put her on the bed. When Mom came downstairs again she found me in a daze and gave me some smelling salts too. Then came release—and hysterics.

Next day when I looked at Vi I got sick. Her face was

nothing but bumps and lumps and all shades of purple and red and black. Her throat had deep black-and-blue dents where I clawed her.

I had almost killed her. But if I had killed her before Mom and the fat man interfered I wouldn't have been sorry. It was the first time I ever whipped Vi. She was scared stiff of me from then on. I never had to fight her again.

The one regret I had was that Mom's Christmas—like everything else in her life—had been spoiled.

My aunts and my mother were not ignorant women. They discussed people and things that happened with considerable intelligence and insight. But I could never get them to listen when I told them about what was happening at school or of anything else that concerned me. They just didn't care. Perhaps they were alienated from me because I was so different in every way from the three of them.

Yet I can't condemn them for that. For them, too, each day was a scuffle, a racking struggle to keep alive. When people are in that situation the problems of a child must seem very unimportant. All that counts is eating and keeping a roof over your head. . . .

2

FROM

A Choice of Weapons

by Gordon Parks

(1912–   )

*The youth of Gordon Parks provides a good example of
how a childhood of violence and hatred can in turn breed
more anger and violence within the child. But Parks' early
upbringing also instilled in him a desire to try to "beat
the system," to grow up and succeed in spite of the apparent futility of the struggle. The significance of the title
of his book, then, is that Parks was presented with a choice
of how to wage his personal fight: whether to lash out bit-
terly and violently, without reason and direction, or to
channel his energies into a meaningful, positive effort. It
is a choice that, at one time or another, every Negro
faces today.*

*Brought up in a small Kansas town in the early 1900's,
Gordon Parks was sent to live with his sister and brother-
in-law after his mother died. His premonition that living
with them was an impermanent state proved to be correct. He left after a bitter argument. What followed was
a succession of temporary jobs—piano player, bellhop,
waiter, basketball player—until he began his career as a*

professional photographer by buying a cheap camera and taking pictures of anything and everything he saw.

Parks has been a staff photographer for Life Magazine *since 1949. He has written and photographed award-winning stories on subjects such as the Black Muslims and the plight of an underprivileged boy named Flavio. He is also a composer whose music has been performed in major cities.*

In the following selection he recalls the fears and hopes of his childhood in Kansas during the second decade of the twentieth century.

THE FULL meaning of my mother's death had settled over me before they lowered her into the grave. They buried her at two-thirty in the afternoon; now, at nightfall, our big family was starting to break up. Once there had been fifteen of us and, at sixteen, I was the youngest. There was never much money, so now my older brothers and sisters were scraping up enough for my coach ticket north. I would live in St. Paul, Minnesota, with my sister Maggie Lee, as my mother had requested a few minutes before she died.

Poppa, a good quiet man, spent the last hours before our parting moving aimlessly about the yard, keeping to himself and avoiding me. A sigh now and then belied his outer calm. Several times I wanted to say that I was sorry to be going, and that I would miss him very much. But the silence that had always lain between us prevented this. Now I realized that probably he hadn't spoken more than a few thousand words to me during my entire childhood. It was always: "Mornin', boy"; "Git you chores done, boy"; "Goodnight, boy." If I asked for a dime or nickel, he would look beyond me for a moment, grunt, then dig through the nuts and bolts in his blue jeans and hand me the money. I loved him in spite of his silence.

For his own reasons Poppa didn't go to the depot, but

as my sister and I were leaving he came up, a cob pipe jutting from his mouth, and stood sideways, looking over the misty Kansas countryside. I stood awkwardly waiting for him to say something. He just grunted—three short grunts. "Well," Maggie Lee said nervously, "won't you be kissin' your poppa goodbye?" I picked up my cardboard suitcase, turned and kissed his stubby cheek and started climbing into the taxicab. I was halfway in when his hand touched my shoulder. "Boy, remember your momma's teachin'. . . . You'll be all right. Just you remember her teachin'. . . ." I promised, then sat back in the Model T taxi. As we rounded the corner, Poppa was already headed for the hog pens. It was feeding time.

Our parents had filled us with love and a staunch Methodist religion. We were poor, though I did not know it at the time; the rich soil surrounding our clapboard house had yielded the food for the family. And the love of this family had eased the burden of being black. But there were segregated schools and warnings to avoid white neighborhoods after dark. I always had to sit in the peanut gallery (the Negro section) at the movies. We weren't allowed to drink soda in the drugstore in town. I was stoned and beaten and called "nigger," "black boy," "darky," "shine." These indignities came so often I began to accept them as normal. Yet I always fought back. Now I considered myself lucky to be alive; three of my close friends had already died of senseless brutality, and I was lucky that I hadn't killed someone myself. Until the very day that I left Fort Scott on that train for the North, there had been a fair chance of being shot or perhaps beaten to death. I could easily have been murdered by some violent member of my own race. There had been a lot of killing in the border states of Kansas, Oklahoma and Missouri, more than I cared to remember.

I was nine years old when the Tulsa riots took place in 1921. Whites had invaded the Negro neighborhood, which turned out to be an armed camp. Many white Tulsans were killed, and rumors had it that the fight would spread into Kansas and beyond. About this time a grown cousin of mine decided to go south to work in a mill. My mother, knowing his hot temper, pleaded with him not to go, but he caught a freight going south. Months passed and we had no word of him. Then one day his name flashed across the nation as one of the most-wanted men in the country. He had killed a white mill-hand who spat in his face and called him "nigger." He killed another white man while fleeing the scene and shot another on the viaduct between Kansas City, Missouri, and Kansas City, Kansas.

I asked Momma questions she couldn't possibly answer. Would they catch him? Would he be lynched? Where did she think he was hiding? How long did she think he could hold out? She knew what all the rest of us knew, that he would come back to our house if it was possible.

He came one night. It was storming, and I lay in the dark of my room, listening to the rain pound the roof. Suddenly, the window next to my bed slid up, and my cousin, wet and cautious, scrambled through the opening. I started to yell as he landed on my bed, but he quickly covered my mouth with his hand, whispered his name, and cautioned me into silence. I got out of bed and followed him. He went straight to Momma's room, kneeled down and shook her awake. "Momma Parks," he whispered, "it's me, it's me. Wake up." And she awoke easily and put her hand on his head. "My Lord, son," she said, "you're in such bad trouble." Then she sat upon the side of the bed and began to pray over him. After she had finished, she tried to persuade him to give himself up. "They'll kill you, son. You can't run forever." But he refused. Then, going to our old icebox, he filled a sack with food and went back out my window into the cornfield.

None of us ever saw or heard of him again. And I would lie awake nights wondering if the whites had killed my cousin, praying that they hadn't. I remembered the huge sacks of peanut brittle he used to bring me and the rides he gave me on the back of his battered motorcycle. And my days were full of fantasies in which I helped him escape imaginary white mobs.

When I was eleven, I became possessed of an exaggerated fear of death. It started one quiet summer afternoon with an explosion in the alley behind our house. I jumped up from under a shade tree and tailed Poppa toward the scene. Black smoke billowed skyward, a large hole gaped in the wall of our barn and several maimed chickens and a headless turkey flopped about on the ground. Then Poppa stopped and muttered, "Good Lord." I clutched his overalls and looked. A man, or what was left of him, was strewn about in three parts. A gas main he had been repairing had somehow ignited and blown everything around it to bits.

Then once, with two friends, I had swum along the bottom of the muddy Marmaton River, trying to locate the body of a Negro man. We had been promised fifty cents apiece by the same white policeman who had shot him while he was in the water trying to escape arrest. The dead man had been in a crap game with several others who had managed to get away. My buddy, Johnny Young, was swimming beside me; we swam with ice hooks which we were to use for grappling. The two of us touched the corpse at the same instant. Fear streaked through me and the memory of his bloated body haunted my dreams for nights.

One night at the Empress Theater, I sat alone in the peanut gallery watching a motion picture, *The Phantom of the Opera*. When the curious heroine, against Lon Chaney's warning, snatched away his mask, and the skull of death filled the screen, I screamed out loud and ran out of the theater. I didn't stop until I reached home, crying to Momma, "I'm going to die! I'm going to die."

Momma, after several months of cajoling, had all but destroyed this fear when another cruel thing happened. A Negro gambler called Captain Tuck was mysteriously killed on the Frisco tracks. Elmer Kinard, a buddy, and I had gone to the Cheney Mortuary out of youthful, perhaps morbid curiosity. Two white men, standing at the back door where bodies were received, smiled mischievously and beckoned to us. Elmer was wise and ran, but they caught me. "Come on in, boy. You want to see Captain Tuck, don't you?"

"No, no," I pleaded. "No, no, let me go."

The two men lifted me through the door and shoved me into a dark room. "Cap'n Tuck's in here, boy. You can say hello to him." The stench of embalming fluid mixed with fright. I started vomiting, screaming and pounding the door. Then a smeared light bulb flickered on and, there before me, his broken body covering the slab, was Captain Tuck. My body froze and I collapsed beside the door.

After they revived me and put me on the street, I ran home with the old fear again running the distance beside me. My brother Clem evened the score with his fists the next day, but from then on Poppa proclaimed that no Parks would ever be caught dead in Cheney's. "The Koonantz boys will do all our burying from now on," he told Orlando Cheney.

Another time, I saw a woman cut another woman to death. There were men around, but they didn't stop it. They all stood there as if they were watching a horror movie. Months later, I would shudder at the sight of Johnny Young, one of my closest buddies, lying, shot to death, at the feet of his father and the girl he loved. His murderer had been in love with the same girl. And not long after, Emphry Hawkins, who had helped us bear Johnny's coffin, was also shot to death.

As the train whistled through the evening, I realized that only hours before, during what seemed like a bottomless night, I had left my bed to sleep on the floor beside my mother's coffin. It was, I knew now, a final attempt to destroy this fear of death.

But in spite of the memories, I would miss this Kansas land that I was leaving. The great prairies filled with green and cornstalks; the flowering apple trees, the tall elms and oaks bordering the streams that gurgled and the rivers that rolled quiet. The summers of long, sleepy days for fishing, swimming and snatching crawdads from beneath the rocks. The endless tufts of high clouds billowing across the heavens. The butterflies to chase through grass high as the chin. The swallowtails, bobolinks and robins. Nights filled with soft laughter, with fireflies and restless stars, and the winding sound of the cricket rubbing dampness from its wing. The silver of September rain, the orange-red-brown Octobers and Novembers, and the white Decembers with the hungry smells of hams and pork butts curing in the smokehouses. Yet as the train sped along, the telegraph poles whizzing toward and past us, I had a feeling that I was escaping a doom which had already trapped the relatives and friends I was leaving behind. For, although I was departing from this beautiful land, it would be impossible ever to forget the fear, hatred and violence that Negroes had suffered upon it.

It was all behind me now. By the next day, there would be what my mother had called "another kind of world, one with more hope and promising things." She had said, "Make a man of yourself up there. Put something into it, and you'll get something out of it." It was her dream for me. When I stepped onto the chilly streets of St. Paul, Minnesota, two days later, I was determined to fulfill that dream.

I had never met my brother-in-law, and his handshake told me that I was to be tolerated rather than accepted.

He was nearly white in color, big and fierce-looking. His whole person seemed formidable. His only words to me that first evening were about things I should not do in his house.

It was a nice house—two-storied, handsomely middle-class, with large, comfortable rooms. And that night, lying in bed, I marveled at the hundreds of deer leaping the bushes on the wallpaper around me, and my thoughts were charged with vague imaginings of the future. Yet I felt that whatever security lay ahead would be of my own making. There was no feeling of permanence in the softness of the ornate bed. I sensed that this was to be an uneasy stopover, and that it would be necessary to move on before long.

"Cut off your lamp! Electric light cost money, boy!" It was my brother-in-law outside the door. I didn't answer. I thought it better to remain silent, but I switched off the light and listened to him lumber down the hall. But, in spite of the long coach ride, I was restless and couldn't sleep. A few minutes later, my sister sneaked in the door with a handful of gingersnaps and a glass of milk and placed them on my night table. "Don't worry. Everything will work out all right," she whispered, then she slipped back into the hallway.

Even on this first night, I had bad feeling for this man. It was the kind of feeling I had for the whites whose indignities had pushed me to the edge of violence, whose injustices toward me had created one emotional crisis after another, all because my skin was black. My mind shifted back to those mornings when I stood before the cracked mirror in our house and wondered why God had made me black, and I remembered the dream I once had of being white, with skin so flabby and loose that I attempted to pull it into shape, to make it fit, only to awaken and find myself clutching at my underwear. But now I knew I was black and that I would always be black.

At fourteen, in the black-and-white world of Kansas, anyone whiter than I became my enemy. I had grown rebellious and once, while in a fit of temper, I knocked my crippled brother Leroy, who was a couple of shades lighter than I, to the floor. Immediately ashamed, I reached down to help him. He smiled and waved me aside, and I ran from the room crying. It hurt to learn several days later that he had known for months that he was incurably ill. Just before he died, the following winter, he called me to his bedside.

"Pedro," he said, using his favorite nickname for me, "for the life of me I don't know why you're so mad at the world. You can't whip it the way you're going. It's too big. If you're going to fight it, use your brain. It's got a lot more power than your fists." Before sleep came that night in St. Paul, it was clear to me that such reasoning was needed if I was to cope with my brother-in-law's hostility.

I awoke early the next day, dressed and went out of doors, eager for a look at the new surroundings. The morning was already brisk and alive, with sunshine full upon the big porch. The tree-lined avenue seemed clean and beautiful. The leaves, yielding to the first frosts, had taken on the golds and oranges of autumn. Stretching full length upon the steps, I was suddenly thankful to be in this bright new land.

People were now on the street, moving with the quickness that autumn mornings enforce. I thought that I too would have to move much faster here; otherwise I would be left behind. . . .

3

FROM

Go Up for Glory

by Bill Russell as told to William McSweeny

(1934–   )

Bill Russell's father was wretchedly unhappy living in Louisiana in the 1930's and early 1940's when Bill was a young boy, so he moved his family to California and, hopefully, a new life.

Bill started to play basketball in high school when a teacher encouraged him to try out for the Jay Vees. Recalls Russell: "I believe that man saved me from becoming a juvenile delinquent. If I hadn't had basketball, all of my energies and frustrations would surely have been carried in some other direction."

Six-foot ten-inch Russell accepted an athletic scholarship to the University of San Francisco. He won a gold medal for the United States at the 1956 Olympics in Melbourne after which he enjoyed a spectacularly successful decade as a Boston Celtic.

Russell wrote Go Up for Glory *at the height of his basketball career. In the following selection he relates his attempts to grapple with the indignities and humiliations and double standards that were as much a part of*

*his boyhood life in California as they had been in Louisi-
ana.*

IN THE prewar period of the thirties and early forties,
growing up in the Deep South did not have as disturbing
an effect on me as visiting it in 1944, or 1956, or 1962.
When you're a kid, you just never realize that there is a
tremendous basic difference between mere existence and
freedom.

At least, I didn't.

I was just a kid who liked his friends and loved his
mother and father and brother and scuffed along the dirt
road, laughing on my way to a barn that was converted
into a school.

Still, there was something deep and underlying—a dis-
quieting factor—the exact nature of which I am probably
still not fully aware. I remember I was fascinated with
the trains that went by and spent many afternoons at the
fence watching and waving at the engineers. Twenty
years later, I spent a good portion of my first salary on an
extensive layout of electric trains. Perhaps to satisfy a
promise I never knew I made. Perhaps to reach a goal I
never knew I set. Perhaps. The trains have been played
with by many friends since. Then, finally, I put them away.
I wonder if perhaps it wasn't closing a chapter in my life.

My father, Charles Russell, had a job in a paper bag
factory. It was what we in the Black South called "a
Negro job." There was advancement, but it was limited.

Charlie Russell was not a man who was ever going to be
kept back, however, and because he was a man, he broke
the bonds eventually and left, moving first to Detroit
and finally to California.

There were things a man simply could not tolerate
in Louisiana.

Flashing memories come back, memories more bitter
now than the events themselves, because at the moment

of occurrence these insults seemed to be absolute facts of existence, which couldn't be overcome. It was a little like being afloat and slowly drowning in a vast sea of tar.

Once we went to the ice house and the attendant just let us sit in the car for fifteen or twenty minutes while he talked to another white man. That man drove off and another car came along and the attendant went to wait on those people, so my father began driving off.

The attendant ran over to my Dad's window and said:

"Don't you ever try to do that, boy. Unless you want to get shot."

He had a big gun.

My dad picked up a tire iron and got out of the car and the red-neck just turned and ran for his life and my heart overflowed with wonder and pride for my father. It does to this moment when I look back to what he was facing.

But Louisiana wasn't the place for him.

There were other things you just couldn't cope with because you couldn't stand up to them, face to face.

My mother, Katie, was a gentle woman. In that time, women affected modified riding habits as stylish street clothes. Katie was awfully proud of her suit, but one day she was shopping in Monroe and a cop came up to her and said:

"Who do you think you are, nigger? Dressed like a white woman. Get out of town before sundown or I'll throw you in jail."

My mother came home in a state of shock.

The memory lingers on a five-year-old boy who watched that woman sitting in the kitchen of our home, trying to understand, trying to comprehend this unwarranted viciousness.

Faced with this—and being a man and the head of the house—my father struck out for freedom. He went to Oakland, California. We remained behind in Monroe until our father was able to send for us.

It was not all insult and injury by any means. My brother Charlie and I had our laughs as well as our tears.

To this day, I still chuckle at one gag we pulled. A peglegged man with an enormously fat wife was a regular visitor to our home. Fascinated with ghosts, they would spend hours discussing the more recent "appearances" of strange images in the district.

One particular evening, they talked on and on, late into the night. Charlie and I pulled off our bed-sheets, finally, and went down the road to wait. Eventually the pegleg man and the fat wife ended their visit. When they came along past our bush, we jumped out, going "who-who-whooo."

Did you ever see a man with a pegleg race a fat wife?

But being a Negro in Louisiana can have its drawbacks.

My brother and I went down to look at a golf course. We weren't planning to play. We knew better.

We had never seen one, so we just went to look over the fence.

Now, we were walking home and throwing stones at each other—not maliciously, just pebbles that we were skipping back and forth—and a guy came by in his car and a pebble hit it.

He chased us all over the backroads. We couldn't get away from him. He finally caught me on the edge of a field. I was seven years old and winded, but I was ready to start running again. He got out of the car and started for me and he said:

"I catch you, nigger, I'm gonna hang you."

The gentleman did not get any closer.

I ran off, half angry, half laughing. Much later in life, I can laugh more. Probably just some poor bum who had a bad day on the golf course.

When my dad was settled in Oakland we received the word—and the money—to come and join him.

The image of the Negro who always eats chicken and

carries his lunch on public transportation is part of American folklore.

I can explain it best by pointing out that all trains in the south were segregated. Negroes couldn't eat on the diner and the only food which would last on a long trip was chicken. So we took our chicken and rode in our segregated car from Louisiana to Little Rock to St. Louis before the rules changed and we could ride in any compartment of the streamliner which took us on to California.

Freedom, a new form of freedom, lay ahead.

Behind was a world which I will continue to fight to my dying breath. Ahead was a world which also had to be fought. And understood. And, in a fashion, conquered.

We moved into the north section of Oakland, sometimes known unaffectionately as "Landlord's Paradise."

It was a regular house with a regular garage, except that eight families were living in the eight rooms and one family was living in the garage. Pigs and sheep and chickens were raised in the backyard. A rotten, filthy hole. A firetrap with light bulbs hanging off uncoated wires.

It was the only place we could find. It was, the landlord said, the war.

War brings out the humanitarians among us.

But Oakland, compared with Louisiana, was Paradise gained.

We finally moved into the project by Cole School. It was an integrated project, integrated to the extent that the whites lived in one section and the Negroes lived in another. We were reasonably happy. We had achieved stature, even by moving into a project, and we remained there until I joined the [Boston] Celtics.

It was in the project yard that I first learned to play basketball. We "organized" a backboard and a ball. Some people "liberate." Our group "organized."

And we lived. My mother and father were both working

in the shipyards and one worked days and one nights, so there was always someone home. It was 1943, a good year, and a happy one.

Beneath it lurked a latent feeling, an instinct which every Negro develops. Talk now of the riot in Watts, Los Angeles, in 1965, but if you want to understand what might have happened in Watts, or anywhere else, understand certain factors which every Negro in this period learned.

It was as much a lesson as any which was taught to us in the fourth grade at the Cole School.

It stood out, harsh and unyielding, a wall which understanding cannot penetrate.

You are a Negro. You are less.

It covered every area. A living, smarting, hurting, smelling, greasy substance which covered you. A morass to fight from.

The Oakland Police at this time were mostly southerners. They worked from a double standard. There are memories which still sear. A Fourth of July celebration at the Park. The kids went up. We were ten, eleven, twelve-year olds. There was an argument between gangs. Not a scheduled riot. A beef between four or five boys. The cops arrested one kid and beat and kicked him as they dragged him off. He was eleven years old.

My brother Charlie wanted to earn some extra money. He was twelve years old. He built a shoe shine box. He bought some polish. He went to shine shoes. The police arrested him for shining shoes. There were white boys doing it, but they were just told to move on. They arrested my brother Charlie because he was a little black boy and they took him to the station and booked him and for all the rest of his life my brother would have a police record.

For shining shoes?

When you are twelve years old?

You are little, but you learn fast. Be off the street by five o'clock. Move fast if you are little and black. Keep moving. Because the police will get you and book you and maybe kick you. Because you are black. And a child wonders: Why did they do it? What does it make me? Am I nothing? Am I a non-person?

The Oakland Police brought in several Negro policemen. But they did not stop any problems. Everyone knew they were policemen who could not arrest white people. The double standard was in force.

What happens?

Reflectively, from the depths of the lessons learned— and, I hope, from the heights of a world partially conquered—these facts come forward:

That police represent society. White Society. The Negro learns to hate authority. And the Negro also learns to hate himself. They are taught through repetition that they are the scum of the earth and they are bad. They have nothing in common with anyone, not even with each other. They are at the bottom of the heap, the bottom of the dung heap.

They become more and more frustrated. They lose respect for themselves and they lose respect for society. Pretty soon you develop a hatred for yourself. And then you lose all association. That is what happened to the Negro in this time, in this place. That is why there has been a Harlem riot and a Detroit riot and a Watts riot.

The burden was placed upon them by the power structure, which broke down their society to the point that there was no identification, no pride.

For me it was different. Oakland was still better than Monroe, Louisiana. And I began reading. I read Richard Halliburton's *Seven Wonders of the World*.

He wrote of the Citadel in Haiti and of Henri Christophe. History has judged Henri Christophe harshly. He was mad. He was a despot. Yet, in my mind, this was the first identification with a Negro who was a leader. Years later, I went to Haiti just to see the Citadel. I saw the deprived of Haiti, the deprivations of the government, the fear of the people. My wife and I were even arrested for being out at night in the back country. I saw fear, felt fear, tasted fear of a different kind, a fear imposed on Negroes by Negroes.

Yet, to this day, I cannot in my mind fix upon Henri Christophe as a bad man. For he was the first hero of my youth. A black man who became the dominant force in a power structure.

Right? Wrong? I do not know. But there are young Negro boys in America this day, this night, who read. And dream.

Later, much later, one night when I was sixteen, I went to bed just a boy. I woke up the next morning proud— so very proud—to be a Negro. The pride has ever since been with me. I could not put my finger on what triggered this emotion. But it was there. I remember it still. So vividly. Walking and going into the kitchen for breakfast with a pride which has never left me. Perhaps, in turn, it gave me the impetus to fight the power structure and to go forward.

It happened. Just that way.

Other things happened as well. One day I came home from school and my mother was not there. She was in the hospital and she was sick.

Two weeks later she was dead.

I never found out why. She was thirty-two and she was dead. My father came home and he woke up Charlie and me and he sat on the bed and he said: "We'll all have to stick together now." I remember I had a warm, cozy feeling. We were all together.

We took her home to Louisiana, home to lie beside her people, in the earth.

While we were there, we went to visit an old friend of my father's.

He was rich. My father was poor. He was white. My father was black.

But they were men together and they fished together and laughed together and of all the men who had come and gone in our lives, Charlie and I always remembered him as my father's friend, as the man of whom my father and mother always spoke warmly.

We went to visit him and they talked while my brother and I sat there and then he said:

"Yeah, Charlie. You always were a good nigger."

It comes back to me even now. The cold whiplash of an anger, of a frustration.

He was my father's friend.

They fished together. They laughed together. They were men together.

But "Charlie was always a good nigger."

In front of his children. Powerless to do anything. Powerless to answer here in the Deep South—the Black South—of Louisiana.

We left our "friend" and went home.

4

FROM

The Autobiography of Malcolm X

with the assistance of Alex Haley

(1925–1965)

Malcolm Little, the son of the Reverend Earl Little, was born on May 19, 1925 in Omaha, Nebraska. His was a poor family with several children, a father who died when the children were still young, and a mother who left her children to shift for themselves.

Malcolm was in reform school before he was thirteen. Several years later he was arrested for theft, but not before he had been labeled as a dope peddler, hoodlum and pimp.

In prison, Malcolm embraced the Muslim religion and at the same time developed a passionate hatred for the "devil white man." Taking the name of Malcolm X, he became a devout follower of Elijah Muhammad whose racist doctrine preached the complete segregation of the races.

Before long Malcolm X tempered his views and was dropped from Muhammad's select clique. He formed a splinter group which roused the hostility of his former leader. From that time on, Malcolm X was a man marked for death. On February 21, 1965, while he was speaking

*in Manhattan, he was gunned down by three members of
Elijah Muhammad's Black Muslims.*

*The Autobiography of Malcolm X was written shortly
before his death. It is not hard to understand his bitterness
when we read of his boyhood years.*

THERE we were. My mother was thirty-four years old
now, with no husband, no provider or protector to take
care of her eight children. But some kind of a family
routine got going again. And for as long as the first insurance money lasted, we did all right.

Wilfred, who was a pretty stable fellow, began to act
older than his age. I think he had the sense to see, when
the rest of us didn't, what was in the wind for us. He
quietly quit school and went to town in search of work.
He took any kind of job he could find and he would come
home, dog-tired, in the evenings, and give whatever he
had made to my mother.

Hilda, who always had been quiet, too, attended to the
babies. Philbert and I didn't contribute anything. We just
fought all the time—each other at home, and then at school
we would team up and fight white kids. Sometimes the
fights would be racial in nature, but they might be about
anything.

Reginald came under my wing. Since he had grown out
of the toddling stage, he and I had become very close. I
suppose I enjoyed the fact that he was the little one, under
me, who looked up to me.

My mother began to buy on credit. My father had al-
way been very strongly against credit. "Credit is the first
step into debt and back into slavery," he had always said.
And then she went to work herself. She would go into
Lansing and find different jobs—in housework, or sewing
—for white people. They didn't realize, usually, that she
was a Negro. A lot of white people around there didn't
want Negroes in their houses.

So she would do fine until in some way or other it got to people who she was, whose widow she was. And then she would be let go. I remember how she used to come home crying, but trying to hide it, because she had lost a job that she needed so much.

Once, when one of us—I cannot remember which—had to go for something to where she was working, and the people saw us, and realized she was actually a Negro, she was fired on the spot, and she came home crying, this time not hiding it.

When the state Welfare people began coming to our house, we would come from school sometimes and find them talking with our mother, asking a thousand questions. They acted and looked at her, and at us, and around our house, in a way that had about it the feeling—at least for me—that we were not people. In their eyesight we were just *things*, that was all.

My mother began to receive two checks—a Welfare check and, I believe, a widow's pension. The checks helped. But they weren't enough, as many of us as there were. When they came, about the first of the month, one always was already owed in full, if not more, to the man at the grocery store. And, after that, the other one didn't last long.

We began to go swiftly downhill. The physical downhill wasn't as quick as the psychological. My mother was, above everything else, a proud woman, and it took its toll on her that she was accepting charity. And her feelings were communicated to us.

She would speak sharply to the man at the grocery store for padding the bill, telling him that she wasn't ignorant, and he didn't like that. She would talk back sharply to the state Welfare people, telling them that she was a grown woman, able to raise her children, that it wasn't necessary for them to keep coming around so much, meddling in our lives. And they didn't like that.

But the monthly Welfare check was their pass. They acted as if they owned us, as if we were their private property. As much as my mother would have liked to, she couldn't keep them out. She would get particularly incensed when they began insisting upon drawing us older children aside, one at a time, out on the porch or somewhere, and asking us questions, or telling us things—against our mother and against each other.

We couldn't understand why, if the state was willing to give us packages of meat, sacks of potatoes and fruit, and cans of all kinds of things, our mother obviously hated to accept. We really couldn't understand. What I later understood was that my mother was making a desperate effort to preserve her pride—and ours.

Pride was just about all we had to preserve, for by 1934, we really began to suffer. This was about the worst depression year, and no one we knew had enough to eat or live on. Some old family friends visited us now and then. At first they brought food. Though it was charity, my mother took it.

Wilfred was working to help. My mother was working when she could find any kind of job. In Lansing, there was a bakery where, for a nickel, a couple of us children would buy a tall flour sack of day-old bread and cookies, and then walk the two miles back out into the country to our house. Our mother knew, I guess, dozens of ways to cook things with bread and out of bread. Stewed tomatoes with bread, maybe that would be a meal. Something like French toast, if we had any eggs. Bread pudding, sometimes with raisins in it. If we got hold of some hamburger, it came to the table more bread than meat. The cookies that were always in the sack with the bread, we just gobbled down straight.

But there were times when there wasn't even a nickel and we would be so hungry we were dizzy. My mother would boil a big pot of dandelion greens, and we would eat that. I remember that some small-minded neighbor put it out, and children would tease us, that we ate "fried grass." Sometimes, if we were lucky, we would have oatmeal or cornmeal mush three times a day. Or mush in the morning and cornbread at night.

Philbert and I were grown up enough to quit fighting long enough to take the .22 caliber rifle that had been our father's and shoot rabbits that some white neighbors up or down the road would buy. I know now that they just did it to help us, because they, like everyone, shot their own rabbits. Sometimes, I remember, Philbert and I would take little Reginald along with us. He wasn't very strong, but he was always so proud to be along. We would trap muskrats out in the little creek in back of our house. And we would lie quiet until unsuspecting bullfrogs appeared, and we would spear them, cut off their legs, and sell them for a nickel a pair to people who lived up and down the road. The whites seemed less restricted in their dietary tastes.

Then, about in late 1934, I would guess, something began to happen. Some kind of psychological deterioration hit our family circle and began to eat away our pride. Perhaps it was the constant tangible evidence that we were destitute. We had known other familes who had gone on relief. We had known without anyone in our home ever expressing it that we had felt prouder not to be at the depot where the free food was passed out. And, now, we were among them. At school, the "on relief" finger suddenly was pointed at us, too, and sometimes it was said aloud.

It seemed that everything to eat in our house was stamped Not To Be Sold. All Welfare food bore this stamp to keep the recipients from selling it. It's a wonder we didn't come to think of Not To Be Sold as a brand name.

Sometimes, instead of going home from school, I walked the two miles up the road into Lansing. I began drifting from store to store, hanging around outside where things like apples were displayed in boxes and barrels and baskets, and I would watch my chance and steal me a treat. You know what a treat was to me? Anything!

Or I began to drop in about dinner time at the home of some family that we knew. I knew that they knew exactly why I was there, but they never embarrassed me by letting on. They would invite me to stay for supper, and I would stuff myself.

Especially, I liked to drop in and visit at the Gohannas' home. They were nice, older people, and great church-goers. I had watched them lead the jumping and shouting when my father preached. They had, living with them— they were raising him—a nephew whom everyone called "Big Boy," and he and I got along fine. Also living with the Gohannas was old Mrs. Adcock, who went with them to church. She was always trying to help anybody she could, visiting anyone she heard was sick, carrying them something. She was the one who, years later, would tell me something that I remembered a long time: "Malcolm, there's one thing I like about you. You're no good, but you don't try to hide it. You are not a hypocrite."

The more I began to stay away from home and visit people and steal from the stores, the more aggressive I became in my inclinations. I never wanted to wait for anything.

I was growing up fast, physically more so than mentally. As I began to be recognized more around the town, I started to become aware of the peculiar attitude of white people toward me. I sensed that it had to do with my father. It was an adult version of what several white children had said at school, in hints, or sometimes in the open, which really expressed what their parents had said—that the Black Legion or the Klan had killed my father, and the insurance company had pulled a fast one in refusing to pay my mother the policy money.

When I began to get caught stealing now and then, the state Welfare people began to focus on me when they came to our house. I can't remember how I first became aware that they were talking of taking me away. What I first remembered along that line was my mother raising a storm about being able to bring up her own children. She would whip me for stealing, and I would try to alarm the neighborhood with my yelling. One thing I have always been proud of is that I never raised my hand against my mother.

In the summertime, at night, in addition to all the other things we did, some of us boys would slip out down the road, or across the pastures and go "cooning" watermelons. White people always associated watermelons with Negroes, and they sometimes called Negroes "coons" among all the other names, and so stealing watermelons became "cooning" them. If white boys were doing it, it implied that they were only acting like Negroes. Whites have always hidden or justified all of the guilts they could by ridiculing or blaming Negroes.

One Halloween night, I remember that a bunch of us were out tipping over those old country outhouses, and one old farmer—I guess he had tipped over enough in his day—had set a trap for us. Always, you sneak up from behind the outhouse, then you gang together and push it, to tip it over. This farmer had taken his outhouse off the hole, and set it just in *front* of the hole. Well, we came sneaking up in single file, in the darkness, and the two white boys in the lead fell down into the outhouse hole neck deep. They smelled so bad it was all we could stand to get them out, and that finished us all for that Halloween. I had just missed falling in myself. The whites were so used to taking the lead, this time it had really gotten them in the hole.

Thus, in various ways, I learned various things. I picked strawberries, and though I can't recall what I got per crate for picking, I remember that after working hard all one day, I wound up with about a dollar, which was a whole lot of money in those times. I was so hungry, I didn't know what to do. I was walking away toward town with visions of buying something good to eat, and this older white boy I knew, Richard Dixon, came up and asked me if I wanted to match nickels. He had plenty of change for my dollar. In about a half hour, he had all the change back, including my dollar, and instead of going to town to buy something, I went home with nothing, and I was bitter. But that was nothing compared to what I felt when I found out later that he had cheated. There is a way that you can catch and hold the nickel and make it come up the way you want. This was my first lesson about gambling; if you see somebody winning all the time, he isn't gambling; he's cheating. Later on in life, if I were continuously losing in any gambling situation, I would watch very closely. It's like the Negro in America seeing the white man win all the time. He's a professional gambler; he has all the cards and the odds stacked on his side, and he has always dealt to our people from the bottom of the deck.

About this time, my mother began to be visited by some Seventh Day Adventists who had moved into a house not too far down the road from us. They would talk to her for hours at a time, and leave booklets and leaflets and magazines for her to read. She read them, and Wilfred, who had started back to school, after we had begun to get the relief food supplies, also read a lot. His head was forever in some book.

Before long, my mother spent much time with the Adventists. It's my belief that what mostly influenced her was that they had even more diet restrictions than she always had taught and practiced with us. Like us, they were against eating rabbit and pork; they followed the Mosaic dietary laws. They ate nothing of the flesh without a split hoof, or that didn't chew a cud. We began to go with my

mother to the Adventist meetings that were held further
out in the country. For us children, I know that the major
attraction was the good food they served. But we listened,
too. There were a handful of Negroes, from small towns in
the area, but I would say that it was ninety-nine percent
white people. The Adventists felt that we were living at the
end of time, that the world soon was coming to an end.
But they were the friendliest white people I had ever seen.
In some ways, though, we children noticed, and, when we
were back at home, discussed that they were different
from us—such as the lack of enough seasoning in their
food, and the different way that white people smelled.

5

FROM

The Long Shadow of Little Rock

by Daisy Bates

Elizabeth Eckford was one of the Negro pupils to whom Little Rock's Central High School reluctantly opened its doors in the now famous integration showdown of 1957. The colored children had originally planned to enter the school in a group, but with racial tensions beyond the danger level, plans were suddenly changed. Elizabeth somehow was never notified of this change. Thus it came to pass that she was left completely alone to face the full fury of the rabid mob that had gathered outside the school. The experience left her near hysteria and it was a long time before she was able to recount the episode. The following selection is her account of the near-tragic incident as told to Daisy Bates.

Miss Eckford graduated from Central High School in 1960. She attended Knox University in Galesburg, Illinois for one year, then transferred to Central State College in Wilberforce, Ohio.

"THE day before we were to go in, we met Superintendent Blossom at the school board office. He told us what the mob might say and do but he never told us we wouldn't have any protection. He told our parents not to come because he wouldn't be able to protect the children if they did.

"That night I was so excited I couldn't sleep. The next morning I was about the first one up. While I was pressing my black and white dress—I had made it to wear on the first day of school—my little brother turned on the TV set. They started telling about a large crowd gathered at the school. The man on TV said he wondered if we were going to show up that morning. Mother called from the kitchen, where she was fixing breakfast. 'Turn that TV off!' She was so upset and worried. I wanted to comfort her, so I said, 'Mother, don't worry.'

"Dad was walking back and forth, from room to room, with a sad expression. He was chewing on his pipe and he had a cigar in his hand, but he didn't light either one. It would have been funny, only he was nervous.

"Before I left home Mother called us into the living-room. She said we should have a word of prayer. Then I caught the bus and got off a block from the school. I saw a large crowd of people standing across the street from the soldiers guarding Central. As I walked on, the crowd suddenly got very quiet. Superintendent Blossom had told us to enter by the front door. I looked at all the people and thought, 'Maybe I will be safer if I walk down the block to the front entrance behind the guards.'

"At the corner I tried to pass through the long line of guards around the school so as to enter the grounds behind them. One of the guards pointed across the street. So I pointed in the same direction and asked whether he meant for me to cross the street and walk down. He nodded 'yes.' So I walked across the street conscious of the crowd that stood there, but they moved away from me.

"For a moment all I could hear was the shuffling of their feet. Then someone shouted, 'Here she comes, get ready!' I moved away from the crowd on the sidewalk and into the street. If the mob came at me I could then cross back over so the guards could protect me.

"The crowd moved in closer and then began to follow me, calling me names. I still wasn't afraid. Just a little bit nervous. Then my knees started to shake all of a sudden and I wondered whether I could make it to the center entrance a block away. It was the longest block I ever walked in my whole life.

"Even so, I still wasn't too scared because all the time I kept thinking that the guards would protect me.

"When I got right in front of the school, I went up to a guard again. But this time he just looked straight ahead and didn't move to let me pass him. I didn't know what to do. Then I looked and saw that the path leading to the front entrance was a little further ahead. So I walked until I was right in front of the path to the front door.

"I stood looking at the school—it looked so big! Just then the guards let some white students go through.

"The crowd was quiet. I guess they were waiting to see what was going to happen. When I was able to steady my knees, I walked up to the guard who had let the white students in. He too didn't move. When I tried to squeeze past him, he raised his bayonet and then the other guards closed in and they raised their bayonets.

"They glared at me with a mean look and I was very frightened and didn't know what to do. I turned around and the crowd came toward me.

"They moved closer and closer. Somebody started yelling, 'Lynch her! Lynch her!'

"I tried to see a friendly face somewhere in the mob—someone who maybe would help. I looked into the face of an old woman and it seemed a kind face, but when I looked at her again, she spat on me.

"They came closer, shouting, 'No nigger bitch is going to get in our school. Get out of here!'

"I turned back to the guards, but their faces told me I

wouldn't get help from them. Then I looked down the block and saw a bench at the bus stop. I thought, 'If I can only get there I will be safe.' I don't know why the bench seemed a safe place to me, but I started walking toward it. I tried to close my mind to what they were shouting, and kept saying to myself, 'If I can only make it to that bench I will be safe.'

"When I finally got there, I don't think I could have gone another step. I sat down and the mob crowded up and began shouting all over again. Someone hollered, 'Drag her over to this tree! Let's take care of this nigger.' Just then a white man sat down beside me, put his arm around me and patted my shoulder. He raised my chin and said, 'Don't let them see you cry.'

"Then, a white lady—she was very nice—she came over to me on the bench. She spoke to me but I don't remember now what she said. She put me on the bus and sat next to me. She asked me my name and tried to talk to me but I don't think I answered. I can't remember much about the bus ride, but the next thing I remember I was standing in front of the School for the Blind, where Mother works.

"I thought, 'Maybe she isn't here. But she has to be here!' So I ran upstairs, and I think some teachers tried to talk to me, but I kept runing until I reached Mother's classroom.

"Mother was standing at the window with her head bowed, but she must have sensed I was there because she turned around. She looked as if she had been crying, and I wanted to tell her I was all right. But I couldn't speak. She put her arms around me and I cried."

6

FROM

Manchild in the Promised Land

by Claude Brown

(1937–   )

"By the time I was nine years old," recalls the author of this selection, "I had been hit by a bus, thrown into the Harlem River (intentionally), hit by a car, severely beaten with a chain, and I had set the house afire." If any reader is dismayed by this statement, let him prepare himself for a far greater shock in the revelations that follow. And let it be remembered that boyhoods such as Claude Brown's are not remarkable in Harlem or in any of the big-city ghettos on the contrary, they are only too commonplace. That such things as murder, theft, rioting, drug addiction, prostitution, and the like could have become so common in the life of a Harlem youth as to receive mention only in passing is the real horror of this story.

Claude Brown wrote Manchild in the Promised Land *in 1965 when he was twenty-eight years old, and it is remarkable that the Claude Brown who went from one reform school to another, who organized gang wars, who smoked pot and who was an accomplished thief, is the same Claude Brown who became a law student at one of America's leading universities.*

"Run!"

Where?

Oh, hell! Let's get out of here!

"Turk! Turk! I'm shot!"

I could hear Turk's voice calling from a far distance, telling me not to go into the fish-and-chips joint. I heard, but I didn't understand. The only thing I knew was that I was going to die.

I ran. There was a bullet in me trying to take my life, all thirteen years of it.

I climbed up on the bar yelling, "Walsh, I'm shot. I'm shot." I could feel the blood running down my leg. Walsh, the fellow who operated the fish-and-chips joint, pushed me off the bar and onto the floor. I couldn't move now, but I was still completely conscious.

Walsh was saying, "Git outta here, kid. I ain't got no time to play."

A woman was screaming, mumbling something about the Lord, and saying, "Somebody done shot that poor child."

Mama ran in. She jumped up and down, screaming like a crazy woman. I began to think about dying. The worst part of dying was thinking about the things and the people that I'd never see again. As I lay there trying to imagine what being dead was like, the policeman who had been trying to control Mama gave up and bent over me. He asked who had shot me. Before I could answer, he was asking me if I could hear him. I told him that I didn't know who had shot me and would he please tell Mama to stop jumping up and down. Every time Mama came down on that shabby floor, the bullet lodged in my stomach felt like a hot poker.

Another policeman had come in and was struggling to keep the crowd outside. I could see Turk in the front of the crowd. Before the cops came, he asked me if I was going to tell them that he was with me. I never answered. I looked at him and wondered if he saw who shot me. Then his question began to ring in my head: "Sonny, you gonna tell 'em I was with you?" I was bleeding on a dirty floor in a fish-and-chips joint, and Turk was standing there in the doorway hoping that I would die before I could tell the cops that he was with me. Not once did Turk ask me how I felt.

Hell, yeah, I thought, I'm gonna tell 'em.

It seemed like hours had passed before the ambulance finally arrived. Mama wanted to go to the hospital with me, but the ambulance attendant said she was too excited. On the way to Harlem Hospital, the cop who was riding with us asked Dad what he had to say. His answer was typical: "I told him about hanging out with those bad-ass boys." The cop was a little surprised. This must be a rookie, I thought.

The next day, Mama was at my bedside telling me that she had prayed and the Lord had told her that I was going to live. Mama said that many of my friends wanted to donate some blood for me, but the hospital would not accept it from narcotics users.

This was one of the worst situations I had ever been in. There was a tube in my nose that went all the way to the pit of my stomach. I was being fed intravenously, and there was a drain in my side. Everybody came to visit me, mainly out of curiosity. The girls were all anxious to know where I had gotten shot. They had heard all kinds of tales about where the bullet struck. The bolder ones wouldn't even bother to ask: they just snatched the cover off me and looked for themselves. In a few days, the word got around that I was in one piece.

On my fourth day in the hospital, I was awakened by a male nurse at about 3 A.M. When he said hello in a very ladyish voice, I thought that he had come to the wrong bed by mistake. After identifying himself, he told me that he had helped Dr. Freeman save my life. The next thing he said, which I didn't understand, had something to do with the hours he had put in working that day. He went on mumbling something about how tired he was and ended up asking me to rub his back. I had already told him that I was grateful to him for helping the doctor save my life. While I rubbed his back above the beltline, he kept pushing my hand down and saying, "Lower, like you are really grateful to me.". I told him that I was sleepy from the needle a nurse had given me. He asked me to pat his behind. After I had done this, he left.

The next day when the fellows came to visit me, I told them about my early-morning visitor. Danny said he would like to meet him. Tito joked about being able to get a dose of clap in the hospital. The guy with the tired back never showed up again, so the fellows never got a chance to meet him. Some of them were disappointed.

After I had been in the hospital for about a week, I was visited by another character. I had noticed a woman visiting one of the patients on the far side of the ward. She was around fifty-five years old, short and fat, and she was wearing old-lady shoes. While I wondered who this woman was, she started across the room in my direction. After she had introduced herself, she told me that she was visiting her son. Her son had been stabbed in the chest with an ice pick by his wife. She said that his left lung had been punctured, but he was doing fine now, and that Jesus was so-o-o good.

Her name was Mrs. Ganey, and she lived on 145th Street. She said my getting shot when I did "was the work of the Lord." My gang had been stealing sheets and bedspreads off clotheslines for months before I had gotten shot. I asked this godly woman why she thought it was the work of the Lord or Jesus or whoever. She began in a sermonlike tone, saying, "Son, people was getting tired-a y'all stealing all dey sheets and spreads." She said that on the night that I had gotten shot, she baited her clothesline with two brand-new bedspreads, turned out all the lights in the apartment, and sat at the kitchen window waiting for us to show.

She waited with a double-barreled shotgun.

The godly woman said that most of our victims thought that we were winos or dope fiends and that most of them had vowed to kill us. At the end of the sermon, the godly woman said, "Thank the Lord I didn't shoot nobody's child." When the godly woman had finally departed, I thought, Thank the Lord for taking her away from my bed.

Later on that night, I was feeling a lot of pain and couldn't get to sleep. A nurse who had heard me moaning and groaning came over and gave me a shot of morphine. Less than twenty minutes later I was deep into a nightmare.

I was back in the fish-and-chips joint, lying on the floor dying. Only, now I was in more pain than before, and there were dozens of Mamas around me jumping up and screaming. I could feel myself dying in the rising pool of blood. The higher the blood rose the more I died.

I dreamt about the boy who Rock and big Stoop had thrown off that roof on 149th Street. None of us had stayed around to see him hit the ground, but I just knew that he died in a pool of blood too. I wished that he would stop screaming, and I wished that Mama would stop screaming. I wished they would let me die quietly.

As the screams began to die out—Mama's and the boy's —I began to think about the dilapidated old tenement building that I lived in, the one that still had the words "pussy" and "fuck you" on the walls where I had scribbled them years ago. The one where the super, Mr. Lawson, caught my little brother writing some more. Dad said he was going to kill Pimp for writing on that wall, and the way he was beating Pimp with that ironing cord, I thought he would. Mama was crying, I was crying, and Pimp had been crying for a long time. She ran out of the house and came back with a cop, who stopped Dad from beating Pimp.

I told Pimp not to cry anymore, just to wait until I got big: I was going to kill Dad, and he could help me if he wanted to.

This was the building where Mr. Lawson had killed a man for peeing in the hall. I remembered being afraid to go downstairs the morning after Mr. Lawson had busted that man's head open with a baseball bat. I could still see blood all over the hall. This was the building where somebody was always shooting out the windows in the hall. They were usually shooting at Johnny D., and they usually missed. This was the building I loved more than any place else in the world. The thought that I would never see this building again scared the hell out of me.

I dreamt about waking up in the middle of the night seven years before and thinking that the Germans or the Japs had come and that the loud noises I heard were bombs falling. Running into Mama's room, I squeezed in between her and Dad at the front window. Thinking that we were watching an air raid, I asked Dad where the sirens were and why the street lights were on. He said, "This ain't no air raid—just a whole lotta niggers gone fool. And git the hell back in that bed!" I went back to bed, but I couldn't go to sleep. The loud screams in the street and the crashing sound of falling plate-glass windows kept me awake for hours. While I listened to the noise, I imagined bombs falling and people running through the streets screaming. I could see mothers running with babies in their arms, grown men running over women and children to save their own lives, and the Japs stabbing babies with bayonets, just like in the movies. I thought, Boy, I sure wish I was out there. I bet the Stinky brothers are out there. Danny and Butch are probably out there having all the fun in the world.

The next day, as I was running out of the house without underwear or socks on, I could hear Mama yelling, "Boy, come back here and put a hat or something on your head!" When I reached the stoop, I was knocked back into the hall by a big man carrying a ham under his coat. While I looked up at him, wondering what was going on, he reached down with one hand and snatched me up, still holding the ham under his coat with his other hand. He stood me up against a wall and ran into the hall with his ham. Before I had a chance to move, other men came running through the hall carrying cases of whiskey, sacks of flour, and cartons of cigarettes. Just as I unglued myself from the wall and started out the door for the second time, I was bowled over again. This time by a cop with a gun in his hand. He never stopped, but after he had gone a couple of yards into the hall, I heard him say, "Look out, kid." On the third try, I got out of the building. But I wasn't sure that this was my street. None of the stores had any windows left, and glass was everywhere. It seemed that all the cops in the world were on 145th Street and Eighth Avenue that day. The cops were telling everybody to move on, and everybody was talking about the riot. I went over to a cop and asked him what a riot was. He told me to go on home. The next cop I asked told me that a riot was what had happened the night before. Putting two and two together I decided that a riot was "a whole lotta niggers gone fool!"

I went around the corner to Butch's house. After I convinced him that I was alone, he opened the door. He said that Kid and Danny were in the kitchen. I saw Kid sitting on the floor with his hand stuck way down in a gallon jar of pickled pigs' ears. Danny was cooking some bacon at the stove, and Butch was busy hiding stuff. It looked as though these guys had stolen a whole grocery store. While

I joined the feast, they took turns telling me about the riot. Danny and Kid hadn't gone home the night before; they were out following the crowds and looting.

My only regret was that I had missed the excitement. I said, "Why don't we have another riot tonight? Then Butch and me can get in it."

Danny said that there were too many cops around to have a riot now. Butch said that they had eaten up all the bread and that he was going to steal some more. I asked if I could come along with him, and he said that I could if I promised to do nothing but watch. I promised, but we both knew that I was lying.

When we got to the street, Butch said he wanted to go across the street and look at the pawnshop. I tagged along. Like many of the stores where the rioters had been, the pawnshop had been set afire. The firemen had torn down a sidewall getting at the fire. So Butch and I just walked in where the wall used to be. Everything I picked up was broken or burned or both. My feet kept sinking into wet furs that had been burned and drenched. The whole place smelled of smoke and was as dirty as a Harlem gutter on a rainy day. The cop out front yelled to us to get out of there. He only had to say it once.

After stopping by the seafood joint and stealing some shrimp and oysters, we went to what was left of Mr. Gordon's grocery store. Butch just walked in, picked up a loaf of bread, and walked out. He told me to come on, but I ignored him and went into the grocery store instead. I picked up two loaves of bread and walked out. When I got outside, a cop looked at me, and I ran into a building and through the backyard to Butch's house. Running through the backyard, I lost all the oysters that I had; when I reached Butch's house, I had only two loaves of bread and two shrimp in my pocket.

Danny, who was doing most of the cooking, went into the street to steal something to drink. Danny, Butch and

Kid were ten years old, four years older than I. Butch was busy making sandwiches on the floor, and Kid was trying to slice up a loaf of bologna. I had never eaten shrimp, but nobody seemed to care because they refused to cook it for me. I told Butch that I was going to cook it myself. He said that there was no more lard in the house and that I would need some grease.

I looked around the house until I came up with some Vaseline hair pomade. I put the shrimp in the frying pan with the hair grease, waited until they had gotten black and were smoking, then took them out and made a sandwich. A few years later I found out that shrimp were supposed to be shelled before cooking. I ate half of the sandwich and hated shrimp for years afterward.

The soft hand tapping on my face to wake me up was Jackie's. She and Della had been to a New Year's Eve party. Jackie wanted to come by the hospital and kiss me at midnight. This was the only time in my life that I ever admitted being glad to see Jackie. I asked them about the party, hoping that they would stay and talk to me for a while. I was afraid that if I went back to sleep, I would have another bad dream.

The next thing I knew, a nurse was waking me up for breakfast. I didn't recall saying goodnight to Jackie and Della, so I must have fallen asleep while they were talking to me. I thought about Sugar, how nice she was, and how she was a real friend. I knew she wanted to be my girl friend, and I liked her a lot. But what would everybody say if I had a buck-toothed girl friend. I remembered Knoxie asking me how I kissed her. That question led to the first fight I'd had with Knoxie in years. No, I couldn't let Sugar be my girl. It was hard enough having her for a friend.

The next day I asked the nurse why she hadn't changed my bed linen, and she said because they were evicting me.

I had been in the hospital for eleven days, but I wasn't ready to go home. I left the hospital on January 2, and went to a convalescent home in Valhalla, New York. After I had been there for three weeks, the activity director took me aside and told me that I was going to New York City to see a judge and that I might be coming back. The following morning, I left to see that judge, but I never got back to Valhalla.

I stood there before Judge Pankin looking solemn and lying like a professional. I thought that he looked too nice to be a judge. A half hour after I had walked into the courtroom, Judge Pankin was telling me that he was sending me to the New York State Training School for Boys. The judge said that he thought I was a chronic liar and that he hoped I would be a better boy when I came out. I asked him if he wanted me to thank him. Mama stopped crying just long enough to say, "Hush your mouth, boy."

Mama tried to change the judge's mind by telling him that I had already been to Wiltwyck School for Boys for two and a half years. And before that, I had been ordered out of the state for at least one year. She said that I had been away from my family too much; that was why I was always getting into trouble.

The judge told Mama that he knew what he was doing and that one day she would be grateful to him for doing it.

I had been sent away before, but this was the first time I was ever afraid to go. When Mama came up to the detention room in Children's Court, I tried to act as though I wasn't afraid. After I told her that Warwick and where I was going were one and the same, Mama began to cry, and so did I.

Most of the guys I knew had been to Warwick and were too old to go back. I knew that there were many guys up there I had mistreated. The Stinky brothers were up there. They thought that I was one of the guys who had pulled a train on their sister in the park the summer before. Bumpy

from 144th Street was up there. I had shot him in the leg
with a zip gun in a rumble only a few months earlier.
There were many guys up there I used to bully on the
streets and at Wiltwyck, guys I had sold tea leaves as pot.
There were rival gang members up there who just hated
my name. All of these guys were waiting for me to show.
The word was out that I couldn't fight any more—that I
had slowed down since I was shot and that a good punch
to the stomach would put my name in the undertaker's
book.

When I got to the Youth House, I tried to find out who
was up at Warwick that I might know. Nobody knew any
of the names I asked about. I knew that if I went up to
Warwick in my condition, I'd never live to get out. I had
a reputation for being a rugged little guy. This meant that
I would have at least a half-dozen fights in the first week
of my stay up there.

It seemed the best thing for me to do was to cop out on
the nut. For the next two nights, I woke up screaming and
banging on the walls. On the third day, I was sent to
Bellevue for observation. This meant that I wouldn't be
going to Warwick for at least twenty-eight days.

While I was in Bellevue, the fellows would come down
and pass notes to me through the doors. Tito and Turk said
they would get bagged and sent to Warwick by the time
I got there. They were both bagged a week later for
smoking pot in front of the police station. They were both
sent to Bellevue. Two weeks after they showed, I went
home. The judge still wanted to send me to Warwick, but
Warwick had a full house, so he sent me home after two
weeks.

The day before I went back to court, I ran into Turk,
who had just gotten out of Bellevue. Tito had been sent to
Warwick, but Turk had gotten a walk because his sheet
wasn't too bad. I told him I would probably be sent to

Warwick the next day. Turk said he had run into Bucky in Bellevue. He told me that he and Tito had voted Bucky out of the clique. I told him that I wasn't going for it because Bucky was my man from short-pants days. Turk said he liked him too, but what else could he do after Bucky had let a white boy beat him in the nutbox? When I heard this, there was nothing I could do but agree with Turk. Bucky had to go. That kind of news spread fast, and who wanted to be in a clique with a stud who let a paddy boy beat him?

The next day, I went to the Youth House to wait for Friday and the trip to Warwick. As I lay in bed that night trying to think of a way out, I began to feel sorry for myself. I began to blame Danny, Butch and Kid for my present fate. I told myself, that I wouldn't be going to Warwick if they hadn't taught me how to steal, play hookey, make homemades, and stuff like that. But then, I thought, aw, hell, it wasn't their fault—as a matter of fact, it was a whole lotta fun.

I remembered sitting on the stoop with Danny, years before, when a girl came up and started yelling at him. She said that her mother didn't want her brother to hang out with Danny any more, because Danny had taught her brother how to play hookey. When the girl had gone down the street, I asked Danny what hookey was. He said it was a game he would teach me as soon as I started going to school.

Danny was a man of his word. He was my next-door neighbor, and he rang the doorbell about 7:30 A.M. on the second day of school. Mama thanked him for volunteering to take me to school. Danny said that he would have taught me to play hookey the day before, but he knew that Mama would have to take me to school on the first day. As we headed toward the backyard to hide our books, Danny began to explain the great game of hookey. It sounded like lots of fun to me. Instead of going to school, we would go all over the city stealing, sneak into a movie, or go up on a roof and throw bottles down into the street. Danny suggested that we start the day off by waiting for Mr. Gordon to put out his vegetables; we could steal some sweet potatoes and cook them in the backyard. I was sorry I hadn't started school sooner, because hookey sure was a lot of fun.

Before I began going to school, I was always in the streets with Danny, Kid, and Butch. Sometimes, without saying a word they would all start to run like hell, and a white man was always chasing them. One morning as I entered the backyard where all the hookey players went to draw up an activity schedule for the day, Butch told me that Danny and Kid had been caught by Mr. Sands the day before. He went on to warn me about Mr. Sands, saying Mr. Sands was that white man who was always chasing somebody and that I should try to remember what he looked like and always be on the lookout for him. He also warned me not to try to outrun Mr. Sands, "because that cat is fast," Butch said, "When you see him, head for a backyard or a roof. He won't follow you there."

During the next three months, I stayed out of school twenty-one days. Dad was beating the hell out of me for playing hookey, and it was no fun being in the street in the winter, so I started going to school regularly. But when spring rolled around, hookey became my favorite game again. Mr. Sands was known to many parents in the neighborhood as the truant officer. He never caught me in the street, but he came to my house many mornings to escort me to class. This was one way of getting me to school, but he never found a way to keep me there. The moment my teacher took her eyes off me, I was back on the street. Every time Dad got a card from Mr. Sands, I got bruises and welts from Dad. The beatings had only a temporary effect on me. Each time, the beatings got worse; and each time, I promised never to play hookey again. One time I kept that promise for three whole weeks.

The older guys had been doing something called "catting" for years. That catting was staying away from home all night was all I knew about the term. Every time I asked one of the fellows to teach me how to cat, I was told I wasn't old enough. As time went on, I learned that guys catted when they were afraid to go home and that they slept everywhere but in comfortable places. The usual places for catting were subway trains, cellars, unlocked cars, under a friend's bed, and in vacant newsstands.

One afternoon when I was eight years old, I came home after a busy day of running from the police, truant officer, and storekeepers. The first thing I did was to look in the mailbox. This had become a habit with me even though I couldn't read. I was looking for a card, a yellow card. That yellow card meant that I would walk into the house and Dad would be waiting for me with his razor strop. He would usually be eating and would pause just long enough to say to me, "Nigger, you got a ass whippin' comin'." My sisters, Carole and Margie, would cry almost as much as I would while Dad was beating me, but this never stopped him. After each beating I got, Carole, who was two years older than I, would beg me to stop playing hookey. There were a few times when I thought I would stop just to keep her and Margie, my younger sister, from crying so much. I decided to threaten Carole and Margie instead, but this didn't help. I continued to play hookey, and they continued to cry on the days that the yellow card got home before I did.

Generally, I would break open the mailbox, take out the card, and throw it away. Whenever I did this, I'd have to break open two or three other mailboxes and throw away the contents, just to make it look good.

This particular afternoon, I saw a yellow card, but I couldn't find anything to break into the box with. Having some matches in my pockets, I decided to burn the card in the box and not bother to break the box open. After I had used all the matches, the card was not completely burned. I stood there getting more frightened by the moment. In a little while, Dad would be coming home; and when he looked in the mailbox, anywhere would be safer than home for me.

This was going to be my first try at catting out. I went looking for somebody to cat with me. My crime partner, Buddy, whom I had played hookey with that day, was busily engaged in a friendly rock fight when I found him in Colonial Park. When I suggested that we go up on the hill and steal some newspapers, Buddy lost interest in the rock fight.

We stole papers from newsstands and sold them on the subway trains until nearly 1 A.M. That was when the third cop woke us and put us off the train with the usual threat. They would always promise to beat us over the head with a billy and lock us up. Looking back, I think the cops took their own threats more seriously than we did. The third cop put us off the Independent Subway at Fifty-ninth Street and Columbus Circle. I wasn't afraid of the cops, but I didn't go back in the subway—the next cop might have taken me home.

In 1945, there was an Automat where we came out of the subway. About five slices of pie later, Buddy and I left the Automat in search of a place to stay the night. In the center of the Circle, there were some old lifeboats that the Navy had put on display.

Buddy and I slept in the boat for two nights. On the third day, Buddy was caught ringing a cash register in a five-and-dime store. He was sent to Children's Center, and I spent the third night in the boat alone. On the fourth night, I met a duty-conscious cop, who took me home. That ended my first catting adventure.

Dad beat me for three consecutive days for telling what

he called "that dumb damn lie about sleeping in a boat on Fifty-ninth Street." On the fourth day, I think he went to check my story out for himself. Anyhow, the beating stopped for a while, and he never mentioned the boat again.

Before long, I was catting regularly, staying away from home for weeks at a time. Sometimes the cops would pick me up and take me to a Children's Center. The Centers were located all over the city. At some time in my childhood I must have spent at least one night in all of them except the one on Staten Island.

The procedure was that a policeman would take me to the Center in the borough where he had picked me up. The Center would assign someone to see that I got a bath and was put to bed. The following day, my parents would be notified as to where I was and asked to come and claim me. Dad was always in favor of leaving me where I was and saying good riddance. But Mama always made the trip. Although Mama never failed to come for me, she seldom found me there when she arrived. I had no trouble getting out of Children's Center, so I seldom stayed for more than a couple of days.

When I was finally brought home—sometimes after weeks of catting—Mama would hide my clothes or my shoes. This would mean that I couldn't get out of the house if I should take a notion to do so. Anyway, that's how Mama had it figured. The truth of the matter is that these measures only made getting out of the house more difficult for me. I would have to wait until one of the fellows came around to see me. After hearing my plight, he would go out and round up some of the gang, and they would steal some clothes and shoes for me. When they had the clothes and shoes, one of them would come to the house and let me know. About ten minutes later, I would put on my sister's dress, climb down the back fire escape, and meet the gang with the clothes.

If something was too small or too large, I would go and steal the right size. This could only be done if the item that didn't fit was not the shoes. If the shoes were too small or large, I would have trouble running in them and probably get caught. So I would wait around in the backyard while someone stole me a pair.

Mama soon realized that hiding my clothes would not keep me in the house. The next thing she tried was threatening to send me away until I was twenty-one. This was only frightening to me at the moment of hearing it. Every so often, either Dad or Mama would sit down and have a heart-to-heart talk with me. These talks were very moving. I always promised to mend my bad ways. I was always sincere and usually kept the promise for about a week. During these weeks, I went to school every day and kept my stealing at a minimum. By the beginning of the second week, I had reverted back to my wicked ways, and Mama would have to start praying all over again.

The neighborhood prophets began making prophecies about my life span. They all had me dead, buried, and forgotten before my twenty-first birthday. These predictions were based on false tales of policemen shooting at me, on truthful tales of my falling off a trolley car into the midst of oncoming automobile traffic while hitching a ride, and also on my uncontrollable urge to steal. There was much justification for these prophecies. By the time I was nine years old, I had been hit by a bus, thrown into the Harlem River (intentionally), hit by a car, severely beaten with a chain. And I had set the house afire.

While Dad was still trying to beat me into a permanent conversion, Mama was certain that somebody had worked roots on me. She was writing to all her relatives in the South for solutions, but they were only able to say, "that boy must been born with the devil in him." Some of them advised Mama to send me down there, because New York was no place to raise a child. Dad thought this was a good idea, and he tried to sell it to Mama. But Mama wasn't about to split up her family. So I stayed in New York, enjoying every crazy minute.

Mama's favorite question was, "Boy, why you so bad?" I tried many times to explain to Mama that I wasn't "so bad." I tried to make her understand that it was trying to be good that generally got me into trouble. I remember telling her that I played hookey to avoid getting into trouble in school. It seemed that whenever I went to school, I got into a fight with the teacher. The teacher would take me to the principal's office. After I had fought with the principal, I would be sent home and not allowed back in school without one of my parents. So to avoid all that trouble, I just didn't go to school. When I stole things, it was only to save the family money and avoid arguments or scolding whenever I asked for money.

Mama seemed silly to me. She was bothered because most of the parents in the neighborhood didn't allow their children to play with me. What she didn't know was that I never wanted to play with them. My friends were all daring like me, tough like me, dirty like me, ragged like me, cursed like me, and had a great love for trouble like me. We took pride in being able to hitch rides on trolleys, buses, taxicabs and in knowing how to steal and fight. We knew that we were the only kids in the neighborhood who usually had more than ten dollars in their pockets. There were other people who knew this too, and that was often a problem for us. Somebody was always trying to shake us down or rob us. This was usually done by the older hustlers in the neighborhood or by storekeepers or cops. At other times, older fellows would shake us down, con us, or Murphy us out of our loot. We accepted this as the ways of life. Everybody was stealing from everybody else. And sometimes we would shake down newsboys and shoeshine boys. So we really had no complaints coming. Although none of my sidekicks was over twelve years of age, we didn't think of ourselves as kids. The other kids my age were thought of as kids by me. I felt that since I knew more about life than they did, I had the right to regard them as kids. . . .

7

FROM

No Day of Triumph

by J. Saunders Redding

(1906–   )

*So great is the pride of some men that when confronted
by a gross injustice they take upon their own shoulders
the entire burden of righting the wrong. Such a man was
Jay Redding's father, who spent every working day of his
life trying to undo the many falsehoods generally circu-
lated about Negroes. This beautiful vignette illustrates
the fierce determination with which an individual can
seek to vindicate his race—and the clearly inspiring impact of his behavior upon his son.*

*Jay S. Redding was born on the fringe of the South in
Wilmington, Delaware, in 1906. His story is unusual in the
sense that he and the other children in his family received
their education without too much financial struggle. All
were graduated from Northern colleges and one brother
received his LL.D. from Harvard Law School. Jay Redding went to Brown. He is recognized as an eminent so-
ciologist, historian and novelist.*

AS far back as I can remember, it was necessary for my
father to eke out his small government salary by doing all

sorts of odd jobs after his regular hours and his vacations. He belonged to a waiters' association, and frequently he served at dinners, banquets, and parties from early evening until dawn. On these occasions he wore the swallow-tailed coat in which he had been married and the black broadcloth trousers which he had picked up at a second-hand shop. This outfit always amused us, for the trousers did not cover his ankles and his big feet spread beneath them in a truly monumental fashion. The coat had a greenish tinge and fitted across his thick shoulders like a harness. My mother had to sew up the shoulder seams after every use. My father cared little about the appearance of his clothes. "So long as they're clean, children," he used to say, when for reasons of pride we used to fidget with his tie, fold down his collars, and see to it that he was wearing a proper belt in his trousers. Our attentions amused him, and he would wink at our mother and say, "Girl, they've all got your side's pride."

Sometimes he would bring from these parties a satchel bulging with steaks, chicken, butter, rolls, and ice cream; and then we feasted—not because we ever went hungry, but because all this was extra and had to be eaten before it spoiled.

My father always took his annual vacation in the late summer or early fall, for then he could find employment among the farmers a few miles outside the city. He would contract to cut corn or harvest potatoes. Sometimes he stayed in the country, but when he did not, he was always back long after we were in bed and gone again before dawn. Often my brother and I, in the room next the bathroom, would wake up in the night and hear my father thrashing about in the tub and murmuring wearily to my mother, who always waited for him late in the night.

As I look back upon it now, I know that my father was driven by more than the necessity to provide a living for his family. Surrounded by whites both at home and at work, he was driven by an intangible something, a merci-less, argus-eyed spiritual enemy that stalked his every movement and lurked in every corner. It goaded him every waking hour, but he could not get at it, though he felt it to be embodied in almost every white man he met. Be-cause of this, he moved with defensive caution, calculat-ing the effect of every action and every utterance upon his unseen enemy. Every day he won defensive victories, but every day the final victory seemed more impossible. He was up at dawn, painting the trim, repairing the roof, putting out ashes, shoveling snow from the sidewalk. In fifteen years he was never late for his work, and only once did he allow an illness to keep him home. His endurance was a thing of spirit.

But the other necessity was there too, the physical need to provide for a family that soon increased to seven. We were a problem. We helled through our clothes, and espe-cially our shoes. My father mended our shoes with thick leather patches that balled clumsily on the soles. He trimmed our hair. When it seemed safe, he avoided doc-tors' bills by purging us with castor oil, plastering us with goose grease, and swathing us in flannel. I myself was often sick with ruinous colds that threatened a serious illness. I was almost constantly under the care of Dr. Elbert, who spent his time thumping my chest and giving me nauseating medicines. But no saving was too trifling, no economy too stringent for my father to make. Some-times it was a joking matter. Our garbage pail seldom contained anything but vegetable parings and bones, for my mother, too, knew the value of a penny. Indeed, her thrift was generally more effective and yet less severe than my father's. She had a reasonableness in the matter which he lacked. Sometimes she raised objections—futilely, for instance, to my father's spending his vacation harvesting for potatoes or cutting corn. She argued the point of his health, but my father's answer was always the same: "Work wouldn't hurt a man."

When I was fourteen or fifteen, I spent a Saturday on one of these corn-cutting expeditions with him. It was the last weekend of his two-weeks vacation, and he had been working on a farm eight miles out of the city. We left home before daylight and reached the farm just at dawn. It was a large farm, and only a part of it was under cultivation. Before we set to work, the farmer joined us. He was a buck-toothed post of a man, with a skin raw and peeled-looking by the sun. The corn field lay some distance from the house and the land sloped away gently to a flat, rocky strip beyond which the corn field rose abruptly. The brown corn stood in marching rows on the side of the hill. The field had not been cared for. High weeds tangled the rows.

"Well, you overstretched yourself, looks like," the farmer said, looking at the uncut corn on the hill.

My father took off his coat and drew his corn knife from the ground, where he had left it the evening before. I saw his jaw tighten like a fist.

"I'll need a knife for my boy here," he said. "We'll get it done. The weeds will hamper us some, but we'll get it done."

"Maybe you will at that," the farmer said, kicking in a mat of weeds. "Didn' have no time to do nothin' with this crop out here myself. Had another colored feller workin' for me, but he ups an' quits 'bout the time I needed him most. Wasn' much of a loss to me, I don't reckon. He sure was a lazy one. This your boy, hunh?"

"Yes," my father said. He looked past the man. "We'll get it done all right."

"I'm from Missouri," the farmer said.

When he came back with the long-bladed corn knife, he stood for a while and watched us work. I had never cut corn before but it was simply a matter of bending one's back and swinging one's blade as close to the roots as one could. When an armful of stalks was cut, we bound them together and stood them up to finish drying for fodder. The weeds were already giving us trouble. They were wet and tough with dew and they tied themselves around our ankles. But for a while the work did not seem hard to me. My father worked easily, making of bending, swinging, grasping one flowing, rhythmic action.

"The other colored feller sure was a lazy one," the farmer said after a while.

My father did not look up, but I watched the farmer spraddle down the hill and across the rocky gully.

"Damn him," my father said. "Damn him!" It was the only time I ever heard him curse. "Sure. That other colored fellow was lazy. Come on, son. Do you want him to think we're lazy too?"

It began to be hard work cutting uphill, and pretty soon the sun was at us. The weeds grabbed at our blades and we had to hack through them to get at the corn. My father cut very fast and determinedly, paying no attention to me. By nine o'clock my legs were rubbery with fatigue. I could hear my father working the dry, screeching corn somewhere ahead and to the left of me. He made an aspirant sound every time he swung his blade, and this came to me quite distinctly. "Hac. Hac. Hac." I seemed to be floating. My head felt enormously swollen. Bending to the corn, I could feel myself falling, but I had no strength to prevent it. I fell face down in the weeds, struggled up. Then suddenly the earth exploded in my face with blackening, sickening force.

When I came around again, my father was kneeling beside me. His face was gray and hard and his eyes and mouth were like Grandma Redding's. My nose was still bleeding a little and blood was on my shirt and smeared on the damp rag with which my father was stroking my face. He had stuck a twig under my upper lip.

"What's the matter, son?" my father asked. "Feel all right now?"

I spit out the twig. "I can't keep up."

"That's all right. I shouldn't have brought you." He was still stroking my face with the wet, blood-smeared rag. It was unpleasant. I smelled and tasted blood. He looked across the gully toward the house that stood naked and ugly in the broad stroke of the sun. "I'll give that farmer a piece of my mind yet," he said.

"When he said, 'I'm from Missouri,' that's slang," I said. "People say I'm from Missouri when they don't believe you can do something. They say, 'Show me.'"

"I'll show him," my father said.

After lunch I felt strong enough to work again, but my father made me lie under the lip of the hill out of the sun, and all afternoon I listened to the sound of his working moving farther and farther away from me. He finished the field just before dark.

8

FROM

Black Boy

by Richard Wright

(1909–1960)

A child's curiosity can be terribly embarrassing; when that a child is a Negro, and when the object of his curiosity is the baffling question of race, then that child can be even more frustrating to his parents. Richard Wright was such a boy, trying to come to grips with the complexities of issues too difficult—or perhaps too simple—for his parents to solve.

Born in 1909, playwright, fiction writer and journalist, Richard Wright is best known for his brilliant novel, Native Son, and for a book of four novellas, Uncle Tom's Children. For the last fifteen years of his life he lived in Paris because he felt there was less discrimination there than in his homeland. He died in France in 1960.

AT last we were at the railroad station with our bags, waiting for the train that would take us to Arkansas; and for the first time I noticed that there were two lines of people at the ticket window, a "white" line and a "black" line. During my visit at Granny's a sense of the two races had been born in me with a sharp concreteness that would never die until I died. When I boarded the train I was aware that we Negroes were in one part of the train and that the whites were in another. Naïvely I wanted to go and see how the whites looked while sitting in their part of the train.

"Can I go and peep at the white folks?" I asked my mother.

"You keep quiet," she said.

"But that wouldn't be wrong, would it?"

"Will you keep still?"

"But why can't I?"

"Quit talking foolishness!"

I had begun to notice that my mother became irritated when I questioned her about whites and blacks, and I could not quite understand it. I wanted to understand these two sets of people who lived side by side and never touched, it seemed, except in violence. Now, there was my grandmother . . . Was she white? Just how white was she? What did the whites think of her whiteness?

"Mama, is Granny white?" I asked as the train rolled through the darkness.

"If you've got eyes, you can see what color she is," my mother said.

"I mean, do the white folks think she's white?"

"Why don't you ask the white folks that?" she countered.

"But you know," I insisted.

"Why should I know?" she asked. "I'm not white."

"Granny looks white," I said, hoping to establish one fact, at least. "Then why is she living with us colored folks?"

"Don't you want Granny to live with us?" she asked, blunting my question.

"Yes."

"Then why are you asking?"

"I want to *know*."

"Doesn't Granny live with us?"

"Yes."

"Isn't that enough?"

"But does she *want* to live with us?"

"Why don't you ask Granny that?" my mother evaded me again in a taunting voice.

"Did Granny become colored when she married Grandpa?"

"Will you stop asking silly questions!"

"But did she?"

"Granny didn't *become* colored," my mother said angrily. "She was *born* the color she is now."

Again I was being shut out of the secret, the thing, the reality I felt somewhere beneath all the words and silences.

"Why didn't Granny marry a white man?" I asked.

"Because she didn't want to," my mother said peevishly.

"Why don't you want to talk to me?" I asked.

She slapped me and I cried. Later, grudgingly, she told me that Granny came of Irish, Scotch, and French stock in which Negro blood had somewhere and somehow been infused. She explained it all in a matter-of-fact, offhand, neutral way; her emotions were not involved at all.

"What was Granny's name before she married Grandpa?"

"Bolden."

"Who gave her that name?"

"The white man who owned her."

"She was a slave?"

"Yes."

"And Bolden was the name of Granny's father?"

"Granny doesn't know who her father was."

"So they just gave her any name?"

"They gave her a name; that's all I know."

"Couldn't Granny find out who her father was?"

"For what, silly?"

"So she could know."

"Know for what?"

"Just to know."

"But for *what?*"

I could not say. I could not get anywhere.

"Mama, where did Father get his name?"

"Like Granny got hers. From a white man."

"Do they know who he is?"

"I don't know."

"Why don't they find out?"

"For what?" my mother demanded harshly.

And I could think of no rational or practical reason why my father should try to find out who his father's father was.

"What has Papa got in him?" I asked.

"Some white and some red and some black," she said.

"Indian, white, and Negro?"

"Yes."

"Then what am I?"

"They'll call you a colored man when you grow up," she said. Then she turned to me and smiled mockingly and asked: "Do you mind, Mr. Wright?"

I was angry and I did not answer. I did not object to being called colored, but I knew that there was something my mother was holding back. She was not concealing facts, but feelings, attitudes, convictions which she did not want me to know; and she became angry when I prodded her. All right, I would find out someday. Just wait. All right, I was colored. It was fine. I did not know enough to be afraid or to anticipate in a concrete manner. True, I had heard that colored people were killed and beaten, but so far it all had seemed remote. There was, of course, a vague uneasiness about it all, but I would be able to handle that when I came to it. It would be simple. If anybody tried to kill me, then I would kill them first.

When we arrived in Elaine I saw that Aunt Maggie lived in a bungalow that had a fence around it. It looked like home and I was glad. I had no suspicion that I was to live here for but a short time and that the manner of my leaving would be my first baptism of racial emotion.

A wide dusty road ran past the house and on each side of the road wild flowers grew. It was summer and the smell of clay dust was everywhere, day and night. I would get up early every morning to wade with my bare feet through the dust of the road, reveling in the strange mixture of the cold dew-wet crust on top of the road and the warm, sun-baked dust beneath.

After sunrise the bees would come out and I discovered that by slapping two palms together smartly, I could kill a bee. My mother warned me to stop, telling me that bees made honey, that it was not good to kill things that made food, that I would eventually be stung. But I felt confident of outwitting any bee. One morning I slapped an enormous bee between my hands just as it lit upon a flower and it stung me in the tender center of my left palm. I ran home screaming.

"Good enough for you," my mother commented dryly. I never crushed any more bees.

Aunt Maggie's husband, Uncle Hoskins, owned a saloon that catered to the hundreds of Negroes who worked in the surrounding sawmills. Remembering the saloon of my Memphis days, I begged Uncle Hoskins to take me to see it and he promised; but my mother said no; she was afraid that I would grow up to be a drunkard if I went inside a saloon again while still a child. Well, if I could not see the saloon, at least I could eat. And at mealtime Aunt Maggie's table was so loaded with food that I could scarcely believe it was real. It took me some time to get used to the idea of there being enough to eat; I felt that if I ate enough there would not be anything left for another time. When I first sat down at Aunt Maggie's table, I could not eat until I had asked:

"Can I eat all I want?"

"Eat as much as you like," Uncle Hoskins said.

I did not believe him. I ate until my stomach hurt, but even then I did not want to get up from the table.

"Your eyes are bigger than your stomach," my mother said.

"Let him eat all he wants to and get used to food," Uncle Hoskins said.

When supper was over I saw that there were many biscuits piled high upon the bread platter, an astonishing and unbelievable sight to me. Though the biscuits were right before my eyes, and though there was more flour in the kitchen, I was apprehensive lest there be no bread for breakfast in the morning. I was afraid that somehow the biscuits might disappear during the night, while I was sleeping. I did not want to wake up in the morning, as I had so often in the past, feeling hungry and knowing that there was no food in the house. So, surreptitiously, I took some of the biscuits from the platter and slipped them into my pocket, not to eat, but to keep as a bulwark against any possible attack of hunger. Even after I had got used to seeing the table loaded with food at each meal, I still stole bread and put it into my pockets. In washing my clothes my mother found the gummy wads and scolded me to break me of the habit; I stopped hiding the bread in my pockets, and hid it about the house, in corners, behind dressers. I did not break the habit of stealing and hoarding bread until my faith that food would be forthcoming at each meal had been somewhat established.

Uncle Hoskins had a horse and buggy and sometimes he used to take me with him to Helena, where he traded. One day when I was riding with him he said:

"Richard, would you like to see this horse drink water out of the middle of the river?"

"Yes," I said, laughing. "But this horse can't do that."

"Yes, he can," Uncle Hoskins said. "Just wait and see."

He lashed the horse and headed the buggy straight for the Mississippi River.

"Where're you going?" I asked, alarm mounting in me.

"We're going to the middle of the river so the horse can drink," he said.

He drove over the levee and down the long slope of cobblestones to the river's edge and the horse plunged wildly in. I looked at the mile stretch of water that lay ahead and leaped up in terror.

"Naw!" I screamed.

"This horse has to drink," Uncle Hoskins said grimly.

"The river's deep!" I shouted.

"The horse can't drink here," Uncle Hoskins said, lashing the back of the struggling animal.

The buggy went farther. The horse slowed a little and tossed his head above the current. I grabbed the side of the buggy, ready to jump, even though I could not swim.

"Sit down or you'll fall out!" Uncle Hoskins shouted.

"Let me out!" I screamed.

The water now came up to the hubs of the wheels of the buggy. I tried to leap into the river and he caught hold of my leg. We were now surrounded by water.

"Let me out!" I continued to scream.

The buggy rolled on and the water rose higher. The horse wagged his head, arched his neck, flung his tail about, walled his eyes, and snorted. I gripped the sides of the buggy with all the strength I had, ready to wrench free and leap if the buggy slipped deeper into the river. Uncle Hoskins and I tussled.

"Whoa!" he yelled at last to the horse.

The horse stopped and neighed. The swirling yellow water was so close that I could have touched the surface of the river. Uncle Hoskins looked at me and laughed.

"Did you really think that I was going to drive this buggy into the middle of the river?" he asked.

I was too scared to answer; my muscles were so taut that they ached.

"It's all right," he said soothingly.

He turned the buggy around and started back toward the levee. I was still clutching the sides of the buggy so tightly that I could not turn them loose.

"We're safe now," he said.

The buggy rolled onto dry land and, as my fear ebbed, I felt that I was dropping from a great height. It seemed that I could smell a sharp, fresh odor. My forehead was damp and my heart thumped heavily.

"I want to get out," I said.

"What's the matter?" he asked.

"I want to get out!"

"We're back on land now, boy."

"Naw! Stop! I want to get out!"

He did not stop the buggy; he did not even turn his head to look at me; he did not understand. I wrenched my leg free with a lunge and leaped headlong out of the buggy, landing in the dust of the road, unhurt. He stopped the buggy.

"Are you really that scared?" he asked softly.

I did not answer; I could not speak. My fear was gone now and he loomed before me like a stranger, like a man with whom I could never share a moment of intimate living.

"Come on, Richard, and get back into the buggy," he said. "I'll take you home now."

I shook my head and began to cry.

"Listen, son, don't you trust me?" he asked. "I was born on that old river. I know that river. There's stone and brick way down under that water. You could wade out for half a mile and it would not come over your head."

His words meant nothing and I would not re-enter the buggy.

"I'd better take you home," he said soberly.

I started down the dusty road. He got out of the buggy and walked beside me. He did not do his shopping that day and when he tried to explain to me what he had been trying to do in frightening me I would not listen or speak to him. I never trusted him after that. Whenever I saw his face the memory of my own terror upon the river would come back, vivid and strong, and it stood as a barrier between us.

Each day Uncle Hoskins went to his saloon in the evening and did not return home until the early hours of the morning. Like my father, he slept in the daytime, but noise never seemed to bother Uncle Hoskins. My brother and I shouted and banged as much as we liked. Often I would creep into his room while he slept and stare at the big shining revolver that lay near his head, within quick reach of his hand. I asked Aunt Maggie why he kept the gun so close to him and she told me that men had threatened to kill him, white men . . .

One morning I awakened to learn that Uncle Hoskins had not come home from the saloon. Aunt Maggie fretted and worried. She wanted to visit the saloon and find out what had happened, but Uncle Hoskins had forbidden her to come to the place. The day wore on and dinnertime came.

"I'm going to find out if anything's happened," Aunt Maggie said.

"Maybe you oughtn't," my mother said. "Maybe it's dangerous."

The food was kept hot on the stove and Aunt Maggie stood on the front porch staring into the deepening dusk. Again she declared that she was going to the saloon, but my mother dissuaded her once more. It grew dark and still he had not come. Aunt Maggie was silent and restless.

"I hope to God the white people didn't bother him," she said.

Later she went into the bedroom and when she came out she whimpered:

"He didn't take his gun. I wonder what could have happened?"

We ate in silence. An hour later there was the sound of heavy footsteps on the front porch and a loud knock came. Aunt Maggie ran to the door and flung it open. A tall black boy stood sweating, panting, and shaking his head. He pulled off his cap.

"Mr. Hoskins . . . he done been shot. Done been shot by a white man," the boy gasped. "Mr. Hoskins, he dead."

Aunt Maggie screamed and rushed off the porch and down the dusty road into the night.

"Maggie!" my mother screamed.

"Don't you-all go to that saloon," the boy called.

"Maggie!" my mother called, running after Aunt Maggie.

"They'll kill you if you go there!" the boy yelled. "White folks say they'll kill all his kinfolks!"

My mother pulled Aunt Maggie back to the house. Fear drowned our grief and that night we packed clothes and dishes and loaded them into a farmer's wagon. Before dawn we were rolling away, fleeing for our lives. I learned afterwards that Uncle Hoskins had been killed by whites who had long coveted his flourishing liquor business. He had been threatened with death and warned many times to leave, but he had wanted to hold on a while longer to amass more money. We got rooms in West Helena, and Aunt Maggie and my mother kept huddled in the house all day and night, afraid to be seen on the streets. Finally Aunt Maggie defied her fear and made frequent trips back to Elaine, but she went in secret and at night and would tell no one save my mother when she was going.

There was no funeral. There was no music. There was no period of mourning. There were no flowers. There were only silence, quiet weeping, whispers, and fear. I did not know when or where Uncle Hoskins was buried. Aunt Maggie was not even allowed to see his body nor was she able to claim any of his assets. Uncle Hoskins had simply been plucked from our midst and we, figuratively, had fallen on our faces to avoid looking into that white-hot face of terror that we knew loomed somewhere above us. This was as close as white terror had ever come to me and my mind reeled. Why had we not fought back, I asked my mother, and the fear that was in her made her slap me into silence.

Shocked, frightened, alone without their husbands or friends, my mother and Aunt Maggie lost faith in themselves and, after much debate and hesitation, they decided to return home to Granny and rest, think, map out new plans for living. I had grown used to moving suddenly and the prospects of another trip did not excite me. I had learned to leave old places without regret and accept new ones for what they looked like. Though I was nearly nine years of age, I had not had a single, unbroken year of school, and I was not conscious of it. I could read and count and that was about as much as most of the people I met could do, grownups or children. Again our household was torn apart; belongings were sold, given away, or simply left behind, and we were off for another long train ride. . . .

9

FROM

Nigger

by Dick Gregory with Robert Lipsyte

(1932–   )

Dick Gregory was born in the depression year of 1932 into a poverty-stricken family whose male wage earner ran out on a wife and six children. As a child, he can remember watching his mother praying and waiting for his father to come home. Unfortunately, this was a common story, because a major element in the history of the urbanization of the American Negro in the twentieth century is the disintegration of the family unit. But emerging from the chaos of ghetto decadence and promiscuity is the figure of the mother. Whenever a child's life in the slums has a happy ending, it is likely due to the almost savage protectiveness of the Negro mother for her children. In the face of overwhelming social and economic forces she wages a desperate struggle to rescue them—for a short while, at least—from the brutality that threatens to bury them. When every day's experience tempts them to despair and loss of self-respect, she strives to inculcate the values of personal dignity and pride. In many of the selections in this book, and especially in this one, she is the unsung heroine of the story.

Today, Dick Gregory is a successful author, comedian, and civil rights leader. But he finds it hard to forget the deprivation of his early years, and he says quite soberly, "I would turn in all the Dick Gregorys in the world and all the nightclubs and all the money just to go back to those days and find a Daddy there."

LIKE a lot of Negro kids, we never would have made it without our Momma. When there was no fatback to go with the beans, no socks to go with the shoes, no hope to go with tomorrow, she'd smile and say: "We ain't poor, we're just broke." Poor is a state of mind you never grow out of, but being broke is just a temporary condition. She always had a big smile, even when her legs and feet swelled from high blood pressure and she collapsed across the table with sugar diabetes. You have to smile twenty-four hours a day, Momma would say. If you walk through life showing the aggravation you've gone through, people will feel sorry for you, and they'll never respect you. She taught us that man has two ways out in life—laughing or crying. There's more hope in laughing. A man can fall down the stairs and lie there in such pain and horror that his own wife will collapse and faint at the sight. But if he can just hold back his pain for a minute she might be able to collect herself and call the doctor. It might mean the difference between his living to laugh again or dying there on the spot.

So you laugh, so you smile. Once a month the big gray relief truck would pull up in front of our house and Momma would flash that big smile and stretch out her hands. "Who else you know in this neighborhood gets this kind of service?" And we could all feel proud when the neighbors, folks who weren't on relief, folks who had Daddies in their houses, would come by the back porch for some of those hundred pounds of potatoes, for some sugar and flour and salty fish. We'd stand out there on the back porch and hand out the food like we were in charge of helping poor people, and then we'd take the food they brought us in return.

And Momma came home one hot summer day and found we'd been evicted, thrown out into the streetcar zone with all our orange-crate chairs and secondhand lamps. She flashed that big smile and dried our tears and bought some penny Kool-Aid. We stood out there and sold drinks to thirsty people coming off the streetcar, and we thought nobody knew we were kicked out—figured they thought we *wanted* to be there. And Momma went off to talk the landlord into letting us back in on credit.

But I wonder about my Momma sometimes, and all the other Negro mothers who got up at 6 A.M. to go to the white man's house with sacks over their shoes because it was so wet and cold. I wonder how they made it. They worked very hard for the man, they made his breakfast and they scrubbed his floors and they diapered his babies. They didn't have too much time for us.

I wonder about my Momma, who walked out of a white woman's clean house at midnight and came back to her own where the lights had been out for three months, and the pipes were frozen and the wind came in through the cracks. She'd have to make deals with the rats: leave some food out for them so they wouldn't gnaw on the doors or bite the babies. The roaches, they were just like part of the family.

I wonder how she felt telling those white kids she took care of to brush their teeth after they ate, to wash their hands after they peed. She could never tell her own kids because there wasn't soap or water back home.

I wonder how Momma felt when we came home from school with a list of vitamins and pills and cod liver oils the school nurse said we had to have. Momma would cry all night, and then go out and spend most of the rent money for pills. A week later, the white man would come for his eighteen dollars rent and Momma would plead with him to wait until tomorrow. She had lost her pocketbook. The relief check was coming. The white folks had some money for her. Tomorrow. I'd be hiding in the coal closet because there was only supposed to be two kids in the flat, and I could hear the rent man curse my Momma and call her a liar. And when he finally went away, Momma put the sacks on her shoes and went off to the rich white folks' house to dress the rich white kids so their mother could take them to a special baby doctor.

Momma had to take us to Homer G. Phillips, the free hospital for Negroes. We'd stand on line and wait for hours, smiling and Uncle Tomming every time a doctor or a nurse passed by. We'd feel good when one of them smiled back and didn't look at us as though we were dirty and had no right coming down there. All the doctors and nurses at Homer G. Phillips were Negro, too.

I remember one time when a doctor in white walked up and said: "What's wrong with him?" as if he didn't believe that anything was.

Momma looked at me and looked at him and shook her head. "I sure don't know, Doctor, but he cried all night long. Held his stomach."

"Bring him in and get his damned clothes off."

I was so mad at the way he was talking to my Momma that I bit down hard on the thermometer. It broke in my mouth. The doctor slapped me across the face.

"Both of you go and stand in the back of the line and wait your turn."

My Momma had to say: "I'm sorry, Doctor," and go to the back of the line. She had five other kids at home and she never knew when she'd have to bring another down to the City Hospital.

And those rich white folks Momma was so proud of. She'd sit around with the other women and they'd talk about how good their white folks were. They'd lie about how rich they were, what nice parties they gave, what good clothes they wore. And how they were going to be remembered in their white folks' wills. The next morning the white lady would say, "We're going on vacation for two months, Lucille, we won't be needing you until we get back." Damn. Two-month vacation without pay.

I wonder how my Momma stayed so good and beautiful in her soul when she worked seven days a week on swollen legs and feet, how she kept teaching us to smile and laugh when the house was dark and cold and she never knew when one of her hungry kids was going to ask about Daddy.

I wonder how she kept from teaching us hate when the social worker came around. She was a nasty bitch with a pinched face who said: "We have reason to suspect you are working, Miss Gregory, and you can be sure I'm going to check on you. We don't stand for welfare cheaters."

Momma, a welfare cheater. A criminal who couldn't stand to see her kids go hungry, or grow up in slums and end up mugging people in dark corners. I guess the system didn't want her to get off relief, the way it kept sending social workers around to be sure Momma wasn't trying to make things better.

I remember how that social worker would poke around the house, wrinkling her nose at the coal dust on the chilly linoleum floor, shaking her head at the bugs crawling over the dirty dishes in the sink. My Momma would have to stand there and make like she was too lazy to keep her own house clean. She could never let on that she spent all day cleaning another woman's house for two dollars and carfare. She would have to follow that nasty bitch around those drafty three rooms, keeping her fingers crossed that the telephone hidden in the closet wouldn't ring. Welfare cases weren't supposed to have telephones.

But Momma figured that some day the Gregory kids were going to get off North Taylor Street and into a world where they would have to compete with kids who grew up with telephones in their houses. She didn't want us to be at a disadvantage. She couldn't explain that to the social worker. And she couldn't explain that while she was out spoon-feeding somebody else's kids, she was worrying about her own kids, that she could rest her mind by picking up the telephone and calling us—to find out if we had bread for our baloney or baloney for our bread, to see if any of us had gotten run over by the streetcar while we played in the gutter, to make sure the house hadn't burnt down from the papers and magazines we stuffed in the stove when the coal ran out.

But sometimes when she called there would be no answer. Home was a place to be only when all other places were closed.

I never learned hate at home, or shame. I had to go to school for that. I was about seven years old when I got my first big lesson. I was in love with a little girl named Helene Tucker, a light-complected little girl with pigtails and nice manners. She was always clean and she was smart in school. I think I went to school then mostly to look at her. I brushed my hair and even got me a little old handkerchief. It was a lady's handkerchief, but I didn't want Helene to see me wipe my nose on my hand. The pipes were frozen again, there was no water in the house, but I washed my socks and shirt every night. I'd get a pot, and go over to Mister Ben's grocery store, and stick my pot down into his soda machine. Scoop out some chopped ice. By evening the ice melted to water for washing. I got sick a lot that winter because the fire would go out at night before the clothes were dry. In the morning I'd put them on, wet or dry, because they were the only clothes I had.

Everybody's got a Helene Tucker, a symbol of everything you want. I loved her for her goodness, her clean-ness, her popularity. She'd walk down my street and my brothers and sisters would yell, "Here comes Helene," and I'd rub my tennis sneakers on the back of my pants and wish my hair wasn't so nappy and the white folks' shirt fit me better. I'd run out on the street. If I knew my place and didn't come too close, she'd wink at me and say hello. That was a good feeling. Sometimes I'd follow her all the way home, and shovel the snow off her walk and try to make friends with her Momma and her aunts. I'd drop money on her stoop late at night on my way back from shining shoes in the taverns. And she had a Daddy, and he had a good job. He was a paper hanger.

I guess I would have gotten over Helene by summertime, but something happened in that classroom that made her face hang in front of me for the next twenty-two years. When I played drums in high school it was for Helene and when I broke track records in college it was for Helene and when I started standing behind microphones and heard applause I wished Helene could hear it, too. It wasn't until I was twenty-nine years old and married and making money that I finally got her out of my system. Helene was sitting in that classroom when I learned to be ashamed of myself.

It was on a Thursday. I was sitting in the back of the room, in a seat with a chalk circle drawn around it. The idiot's seat, the troublemaker's seat.

The teacher thought I was stupid. Couldn't spell, couldn't read, couldn't do arithmetic. Just stupid. Teachers were never interested in finding out that you couldn't concentrate because you were so hungry, because you hadn't had any breakfast. All you could think about was noontime, would it ever come? Maybe you could sneak into the cloakroom and steal a bite of some kid's lunch out of a coat pocket. A bit of something. Paste. You can't really make a meal of the paste, or put it on bread for a sandwich, but sometimes I'd scoop a few spoonfuls out of the paste jar in the back of the room. Pregnant people get strange tastes. I was pregnant with poverty. Pregnant with dirt and pregnant with smells that made people turn away, pregnant with cold and pregnant with shoes that were never bought for me, pregnant with five other people in my bed and no Daddy in the next room, and pregnant with hunger. Paste doesn't taste too bad when you're hungry.

The teacher thought I was a troublemaker. All she saw from the front of the room was a little black boy who squirmed in his idiot's seat and made noises and poked the kids around him. I guess she couldn't see a kid who made noises because he wanted someone to know he was there.

It was on a Thursday, the day before the Negro payday. The eagle always flew on Friday. The teacher was asking each student how much his father would give to the Community Chest. On Friday night, each kid would get the money from his father, and on Monday he would bring it to the school. I decided I was going to buy me a Daddy right then. I had money in my pocket from shining shoes and selling papers, and whatever Helene Tucker pledged for her Daddy I was going to top it. And I'd hand the money right in. I wasn't going to wait until Monday to buy me a Daddy.

I was shaking, scared to death. The teacher opened her book and started calling out names alphabetically.

"Helene Tucker?"

"My Daddy said he'd give me two dollars and fifty cents."

"That's very nice, Helene. Very, very nice indeed."

That made me feel pretty good. It wouldn't take too much to top that. I had almost three dollars in dimes and quarters in my pocket. I stuck my hand in my pocket and held onto the money, waiting for her to call my name. But the teacher closed the book after she called everybody else in the class.

I stood up and raised my hand.

"What is it now?"

"You forgot me."

She turned toward the blackboard. "I don't have time to be playing with you, Richard."

"My Daddy said he'd . . ."

"Sit down, Richard, you're disturbing the class."

"My Daddy said he'd give . . . fifteen dollars."

She turned around and looked mad. "We are collecting this money for you and your kind, Richard Gregory. If your Daddy can give fifteen dollars you have no business being on relief."

"I got it right now, I got it right now, my Daddy gave it to me to turn in today, my Daddy said . . ."

"And furthermore," she said, looking right at me, her nostrils getting big and her lips getting thin and her eyes opening wide, "we know you don't have a Daddy."

Helene Tucker turned around, her eyes full of tears. She felt sorry for me. Then I couldn't see her too well because I was crying, too.

"Sit down, Richard."

And I always thought the teacher kind of liked me. She always picked me to wash the blackboard on Friday, after school. That was a big thrill, it made me feel important. If I didn't wash it, come Monday the school might not function right.

"Where are you going, Richard?"

I walked out of school that day, and for a long time I didn't go back very often. There was shame there.

Now there was shame everywhere. It seemed like the whole world had been inside that classroom, everyone had heard what the teacher had said, everyone had turned around and felt sorry for me. There was shame in going to the Worthy Boys Annual Christmas Dinner for you and your kind, because everybody knew what a worthy boy was. Why couldn't they just call it the Boys Annual Dinner, why'd they have to give it a name? There was shame in wearing the brown and orange and white plaid mackinaw the welfare gave to 3,000 boys. Why'd it have to be the same for everybody so when you walked down the street the people could see you were on relief? It was a nice warm mackinaw and it had a hood, and my Momma beat me and called me a little rat when she found out I stuffed it in the bottom of a pail full of garbage way over on Cottage Street. There was shame in running over to Mister Ben's at the end of the day and asking for his rotten peaches, there was shame in asking Mrs. Simmons for a spoonful of sugar, there was shame in running out to meet the relief truck. I hated that truck, full of food for you and your kind. I ran into the house and hid when it came. And then I started to sneak through alleys, to take the long way home so the people going into White's Eat Shop wouldn't see me. Yeah, the whole world heard the teacher that day, we all know you don't have a Daddy.

It lasted for a while, this kind of numbness. I spent a lot of time feeling sorry for myself. And then one day I met this wino in a restaurant. I'd been out hustling all day, shining shoes, selling newspapers, and I had goo-gobs of money in my pocket. Bought me a bowl of chili for fifteen cents, and a cheeseburger for fifteen cents, and a Pepsi for five cents, and a piece of chocolate cake for ten cents. That was a good meal. I was eating when this old wino came in. I love winos because they never hurt anyone but themselves.

The old wino sat down at the counter and ordered twenty-six cents worth of food. He ate it like he really enjoyed it. When the owner, Mister Williams, asked him to pay the check, the old wino didn't lie or go through his pocket like he suddenly found a hole.

He just said: "Don't have no money."

The owner yelled: "Why in hell you come in here and eat my food if you don't have no money? That food costs me money."

Mister Williams jumped over the counter and knocked the wino off his stool and beat him over the head with a pop bottle. Then he stepped back and watched the wino bleed. Then he kicked him. And he kicked him again.

I looked at the wino with blood all over his face and I went over. "Leave him alone, Mister Williams. I'll pay the twenty-six cents."

The wino got up, slowly, pulling himself up to the stool, then up to the counter, holding on for a minute until his legs stopped shaking so bad. He looked at me with pure hate. "Keep your twenty-six cents. You don't have to pay, not now. I just finished paying for it."

He started to walk out, and as he passed me, he reached down and touched my shoulder. "Thanks, sonny, but it's too late now. Why didn't you pay it before?"

I was pretty sick about that. I waited too long to help another man.

I remember a white lady who came to our door once around Thanksgiving time. She wore a wooly, green bonnet around her head, and she smiled a lot.

"Is your mother home, little boy?"

"No, she ain't."

"May I come in?"

"What do you want, ma'am?"

She didn't stop smiling once, but she sighed a little when she bent down and lifted up a big yellow basket. The kind I saw around church that were called Baskets for the Needy.

"This is for you."

"What's in there?"

"All sorts of good things," she said, smiling. "There's candy and potatoes and cake and cranberry sauce and"—

she made a funny little face at me by wrinkling up her nose—"and a great big fat turkey for Thanksgiving dinner."

"Is it cooked?"

"A big fat juicy turkey, all plucked clean for you. . . ."

"Is it cooked?"

"No, it's not. . . ."

"We ain't got nothing in the house to cook it with, lady."

I slammed the door in her face. Wouldn't that be a bitch, to have a turkey like that in the house with no way to cook it? No gas, no electricity, no coal. Just a big fat juicy raw turkey.

I remember Mister Ben, the grocery-store man, a round little white man with funny little tufts of white hair on his head and sad look eyes. His face was kind of gray-colored, and the skin was loose and shook when he talked.

"Momma want a loaf of bread, Mister Ben, fresh bread."

"Right away, Richard," he'd say and get the bread he bought three days old from the bakeries downtown. It was the only kind he had for his credit-book customers. He dropped it on the counter. Clunk.

I'd hand him the credit book, that green tablet with the picture of the snuff can on it, to write down how much we owed him. He'd lick the tip of that stubby pencil he kept behind his ear. Six cents.

"How you like school, Richard?"

"I like school fine, Mister Ben."

"Good boy, you study, get smart."

I'd run home to Momma and tell her that the bread wasn't fresh bread, it was stale bread. She'd flash the big smile.

"Oh, that Mister Ben, he knew I was fixin to make toast."

The peaches were rotten and the bread wasn't fresh and sometimes the butter was green, but when it came down to the nitty-gritty you could always go to Mister Ben. Before a Jewish holiday he'd take all the food that was going to spoil while the store was shut and bring it over to our house. Before Christmas he'd send over some meat even though he knew it was going on the tablet and he might never see his money. When the push came to the shove and every hungry belly in the house was beginning to eat on itself, Momma could go to Mister Ben and always get enough for some kind of dinner.

But I can remember three days in a row I went into Mister Ben's and asked him to give me a penny Mr. Goodbar from the window.

Three days in a row he said: "Out, out, or I'll tell your Momma you been begging."

One night I threw a brick through his window and took it.

The next day I went into Mister Ben's to get some bread for Momma and his skin was shaking and I heard him tell a lady, "I can't understand why should anybody break my window for a penny piece of candy, a lousy piece of candy, all they got to do is ask, that's all, and I give."

Epilogue

NINETEEN Negro Americans look back on their childhood in this land of freedom and reluctantly conclude that all men were not given equal opportunity. They realize, to begin with, that Thomas Jefferson never meant to include people with black skin when he wrote that all men were entitled to life, liberty and the pursuit of happiness. In fact, as Richard Hofstadter wryly noted, "the leisure, that made possible [Jefferson's] great writings on human liberty was supported by the labors of three generations of slaves." Moreover, if any one thought emerges from the pages of this book, it is that at *no* time in American history have Negroes been able to feel that these "inalienable rights" were really theirs. Because when they look back they remember, without exception, that at some point, somewhere in the vulnerability of their childhood they were made to feel that to be a Negro—not even necessarily to have a dark skin,—meant somehow to be inferior. And this is true whether they lived in the 1820's or the 1960's.

This is not to say, however, that there is no difference

between the two eras, for indeed, the Civil War did abolish legal slavery. Yet the bullwhip of the slaveholder was never completely eliminated. It was only replaced by more insidious weapons of degradation such as restricted housing, low-paying jobs and poor education. It is true that the Reconstruction Amendments to the Constitution that abolished slavery, assured equal protection under the laws, and gave the right to vote to all persons born or naturalized in the United States, leveled all citizens in theory. It has taken a great deal of time and civil rights legislation, however, to make any real progress toward reducing the social and economic differences between the white majority and the black minority in America today. The fact remains that discrimination still exists, and Negro children still suffer with the knowledge that they are growing up as second-class citizens.

But despite this knowledge, there is a surprising spirit of hope that emerges as a common motif from these autobiographies. It is surprising because it seems more reasonable to expect despair when certainly there is so much to despair of in these chapters. Almost to the last man, however, the authors believe the distemper of racism will one day be a thing of the past.

Admittedly, no one remedy is going to end the barbarity and cruelty that is the consequence of discrimination. But eventually better educational facilities, job opportunities, poverty programs and civil rights legislation may bring us to a time when a book called *Growing Up Black* will be as outdated and pointless as a book called *Growing Up White*.

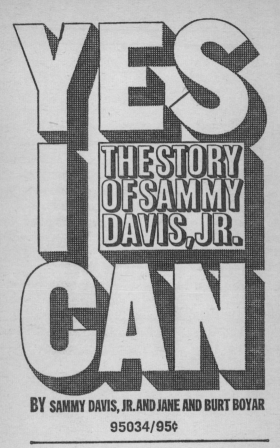

YES I CAN

THE STORY OF SAMMY DAVIS, JR.

CAN

BY SAMMY DAVIS, JR. AND JANE AND BURT BOYAR

95034/95¢

If your bookseller does not have this title, you may
order it by sending retail price, plus 15¢ for mailing
and handling to: MAIL SERVICE DEPARTMENT,
POCKET BOOKS, A Division of Simon & Schuster,
Inc., 1 West 39th St., New York, N.Y. 10018. Not
responsible for orders containing cash. Please send
check or money order.

PUBLISHED BY
POCKET BOOKS
(G 1/9)